My Writing Life

Reflections on my high school hero and literary mentor Ernest "Papa" Hemingway

SEQUEL *to*
The Lion That Swallowed Hemingway

Orest Stocco

My Writing Life

Copyright © 2017 by OREST STOCCO

ISBN 978-1-926442-19-8

Edited by Penny Lynn Cates

Cover Design by Penny Lynn Cates

*For Melanie whose gift of a Hemingway Notebook
inspired this journal on my writing life
and Ernest Hemingway.*

"In truly great writing no matter how many times you read it you do not know how it is done. That is because there is a mystery in all great writing and that mystery does not dissect out. It continues and it is always valid. Each time you re-read you see or learn something more."

Letter to Harvey Breit, 1952
Ernest Hemingway

"The writer battling for canonicity may fight on behalf
of a social class, but primarily each ambitious writer
is out for himself alone and will frequently betray
or neglect his class in order to advance his own
interests, which center entirely upon
individuation."

The Western Canon
Harold Bloom

Note to the Reader

I do not choose the books I write, they choose me; and three years after I wrote *The Lion that Swallowed Hemingway* I was called to write this sequel. I did not know it was going be a sequel, but such is the nature of the creative process; the *daimon* has a mind of its own, and when I was given the title *My Writing Life,* I took the lead and went with it.

"The *daimon* knows how it is done," said the American Gnostic Ralph Waldo Emerson, because the *daimon* is the archetypal spirit of one's own *becoming* and infinitely wiser than our cognitive mind, which is the preoccupying theme of *The Lion that Swallowed Hemingway* and *My Writing Life*; but in my call back to Hemingway, I did not expect to resolve my lifelong fascination with Ernest "Papa" Hemingway as well as my moral obligation to William Somerset Maugham whose novel *The Razor's Edge* called me in high school to become a seeker like Maugham's hero Larry Darrell, and as personal as *My Writing Life* turned out to be, it speaks to the magical healing powers of poetry and literature.

There's a deep mystery to poetry and literature that compels writers to write and readers to read, and in *The Lion that Swallowed Hemingway* and *My Writing Life* I did my very best to bring resolution to this mystery. But I will leave it to the reader to decide whether I have succeeded or not, if one has the patience to follow the logic of my *daimon.*

Happy reading…

Orest Stocco,
Georgian Bay, Ontario
Friday, July 7, 2017

Table of Contents

1. The Immortal Wound

Wednesday, March 1, 2017

He was only twelve or thirteen years old when it happened. "I remember one day I stumbled upon 'The Sleepers'" (a poem by Walt Whitman), said Professor Harold Bloom to Paul Holdengraber at the New York Public Library, "and that was it. That gave the immortal wound…that extraordinary vision of a drowned, heroic swimmer."

"What do you mean when you say immortal wound?" Paul Holdengraber asked, excited by the phrase that alerted him to the mystical power of poetry.

"Well, if a poem pierces you enough in heart and intellect so that you never really get over it, that qualifies as an immortal wound," replied Professor Bloom, and he went on to expand upon the mystifying phrase: "Any poet who wounds you with wonder gives you an immortal wound. "

I didn't have it in me to work on my story, so I went on YouTube to divert myself, and I was strongly nudged to watch the Holdengraber interview with Professor Bloom on his new book *The Anatomy of Influence*, which I had seen once or twice already; but I loved listening to Professor Bloom, who was afflicted with what he called "literary melancholia," talking about poetry and literature. His erudition and "scandalous" memory amazed me.

That was the first coincidence, though I did not see it at the time as a sign directing me back to creative writing; but later in the day when Penny came home from work and we were sitting on our deck having a drink before we went in for dinner (it was "Pancake Tuesday," and she was making the pancakes; I had the bacon in the frying pan ready to go), our neighbor, who was being walked by his two aggressive little terriers, saw us on our deck and came over.

"Well, is your wife anxious over her decision?" I asked. Lenny had told me the other day that his wife had just signed her retirement papers, and I was curious to know if she was anxious about her decision to take an early retirement.

Lenny's wife was the Director of Human Resources with the company she worked for, and "making big bucks" according to Lenny who had retired five years earlier at fifty-five, and I thought his wife's anxiety would be expected; but he said she was okay with it.

"She wants us to go down south as soon as she retires," he said. "We can skip the spring weather and come back in June and work on doing our driveway and landscaping.

They had just built their new retirement home down the street from us, with a double car garage and a forty-foot separate garage to house their fifth-wheeler that they were going to take to the states as soon as his wife retired, and one topic led to another and he told me about a movie he had just seen on Netflix called *Papa Hemingway in Cuba*.

"No kidding?" I said, excited. "*Papa Hemingway* is one of my favorite biographies. That's a personal memoir written by Aaron Hotchner whom Papa Hemingway befriended when he was a young journalist. I'd love to see it. I wonder if it's on YouTube."

"I don't know," Lenny said. "I watched it on Netflix."

We weren't on Netflix, but I learned after our pancake dinner when I went online that *Papa Hemingway in Cuba* wasn't based on Hotchner's biography as I had thought, but on another young American journalist that Papa Hemingway had also befriended in Cuba, and by happy coincidence I did find the movie on YouTube and enjoyed it because it gave me new insights into Ernest Hemingway's life in Cuba with his fourth wife Mary.

Watching *Papa Hemingway in Cuba* excited my curiosity about the movie *Genius*, which was based upon A. Scott Berg's biography *Max Perkins, Editor of Genius* that I had just read the week before, but I couldn't find the movie on YouTube; so I asked Penny if she would enroll us with Netflix, and within the hour I was watching *Genius* on Netflix, a brilliant movie that gave me an inside look at the relationship *Scribner's* famous editor Maxwell Perkins had with three of his most successful authors—Thomas Wolfe, Ernest Hemingway, and F. Scott Fitzgerald, and I enjoyed every moment of it.

There it was, then; the three coincidences—watching Professor Bloom talking with Paul Holdengraber about the immortal wound that Whitman had inflicted upon his soul; the movie *Papa Hemingway in Cuba*; and the movie *Genius*, and I felt a sudden pang of guilt for not making my commitment to creative writing that I had been called upon to make which those three coincidences pointed me to, and I went to bed with Professor Bloom, Thomas Wolfe, Ernest Hemingway, and Scott Fitzgerald on my mind...

The writing life is not an easy life, but I was spared the *daimonic* pull to writing that the three literary giants Wolfe, Hemingway, and Fitzgerald suffered from; mine was a different kind of pull which transcended my call to writing, and I suffered in ways that those three great lions of literature could never have imagined.

But that was precisely what my *daimon* demanded of me with all those coincidences (the initial coincidence was receiving a gift of an *Indigo Hemingway Notebook* from Penny's sister for Christmas, which brought me back to my high school hero and literary mentor who inspired my memoir *The Lion that Swallowed Hemingway*), to write about my own journey of self-discovery that Whitman, Wolfe, Hemingway, and Fitzgerald had also written about; but my poetry and stories would be different, because unlike them I had succeeded in my journey of self-discovery that all creative writers are called upon to write about.

That's why I no longer had the same desperate need to write as the sublime Walt Whitman whose whole life was to complete "Song of Myself," or Thomas Wolfe's desperate quest for the *way* that he never found ("The *way*! The *way*! Do you understand? I'm looking for the way," said his alter ego in *You Can't Go Home Again*), or Ernest Hemingway's irrepressible effort to find "the secret that is poetry written into prose," or F. Scott Fitzgerald's frantic search for the "dust on a butterfly's wings" that his soul-numbing boozing had destroyed; I had found what they all sought through their writing, and I was no longer driven by my *daimon* to complete my journey to wholeness and completeness.

But as much as I love to write, it's hard to sit down at my computer every morning to write, and I have to find ways to keep myself engaged; because the only thing that drives writers to write is their inherent need for wholeness and completeness that writing gives them but which I no longer needed because I had found my true self, and I have to fight off the boredom and depression that could easily possess me if I did not write every day.

I have stories that I've already written but need some editing and revision, and four or five novels also written that need polishing, but ever since my heart surgery eight years ago I no longer have the energy I used to have to work on them, and this pains me. I have two more stories to type up for my book *Sparkles in the Mist and Other Stories*, but I can't seem to muster the desire to complete this book, and I keep putting it off by writing poetry and spiritual musings for my blog, and now this journal on my writing life that I was called to write by my *Hemingway Notebook* that I got from Penny's sister for Christmas.

I've completed my book of poetry *Not My Circus, Not My Monkeys* that I hope Penny, who edits and publishes my books online with Lulu, can have ready for world-wide distribution through Amazon this summer, and I only have one more musing to complete for my fourth volume of spiritual musings called *The Armchair Guru*, so on the whole I'm not as creatively arid as I make out to be; but I am listless, because I remember what it was like getting up at four every morning to write before going to work my trade of taping and/or painting all day and still have energy to spare; but now it's one day at a time, hoping to get a page or two written in the morning and spending the rest of my day doing chores and reading, online research, going for a walk, watching TV, YouTube, and now Netflix movies. I miss the life I used to have before open-heart surgery, and I'm doing my best; but it's not easy.

The most difficult thing is adjustment to my new normal. This is not easy to explain, but I'm trying to illustrate this in my poetry. "The essence of poetry is invention," said Professor Bloom to Paul Holdengraber, quoting his hero Dr. Samuel Johnson, "and by invention he meant discovery," Bloom explained; but discovery of what?

That's what I tried to capture in *Not My Circus, Not My Monkeys*, discovery of the *way* that every writer seeks, whether they know it or not, that mystical path to wholeness and completeness that only the most fortunate will ever find but which their writing discloses each time they create a new poem, story, or novel; which is why they *have* to write.

Some writers find the *way*, like the Sufi mystic Rumi and Emily Dickinson; that's what makes their poetry so difficult to

4

understand. The very nature of the *way* makes it next-to-impossible to apprehend, because it seems to evaporate into a mystical kind of vaporous evanescence every time a writer tries to grasp it. That's why they keep writing.

And when a writer does find the *way* and tries to reveal it, they have to be circumspect, because too much truth can be hard to bear, ergo Emily Dickinson. "The truth must dazzle gradually /Or every man be blind," she wrote, and went on to advise initiates of the *way* to "Tell the truth but tell it slant /Success in circuit lies," which I make every effort to do in my own poetry, like the poem I posted on my spiritual musings blog that was inspired by a contemporary seeker/writer who missed her opportunity: —

Eat, Pray, and Love Some More

Such longing, such effort, such accomplishment,
one adventure after another, always striving
for new *becoming*, and happiness came
when she dared to walk away from
the life she had created, —

An exotic flavor, a new life and new beginning,
and love flowed from the horn of limitless
plenty, but more of the same bred ennui
and she walked away again to satisfy
her deepest longing, —

Onward outward forward, looking, looking,
looking for the magic elixir of her life's meaning,
purpose-driven to find a way through the eye
of the needle—*heavenly kingdom of pure bliss,
desireless desire, her key to freedom,* —

And destiny came calling once more, as life is wont
to do: hair intervention with a strange new creature,
lesbian hair dresser, gifted musician, former addict
and dispossessed, a long way from safety and
security; and she fell in love again with

5

an erotic new flavor, —

On the edge once more, staring into the abyss
of heavenly bliss, all of her instincts screaming NO!
NO! to her feverish longing, but too fat to squeeze
through the eye of the needle she now waits in
spiritual dis-ease for the merciful law of life
to call again and save her from herself.

There's a price to pay to find one's *way*, and a much bigger price to pay when one lives the imperative of the *way*, which I wrote about in *The Pearl of Great Price*; but the real question is not the price that one must pay to find and live one's *way*, but to offer a viable understanding of what the *way* is when one has found it.

I haven't written it yet (it's only an idea that's gaining hold of me each day), but I've been called to write an essay on the *way* for my new book of poetry; and if there is any consistency to how my Muse works with me, I'll be writing this essay once I've written the concluding 100th poem for my new book of poetry, *The Devil's Hindquarter.*

Which brings me to the question of creative writing. Just this morning as I was waiting for the coffee maker to drip my first cup of coffee, I read an essay in Siri Hustvedt's book *A Woman Looking at Men Looking at Women: Essays on Art, Sex, and the Mind,* in which she questions the process of writing. Her essay is called "Why One Story and Not Another," and when I finished reading it I could see that she was no closer to finding an answer than when she started; but it does offer an insight into how deeply mysterious the writing process is.

Siri Hustvedt tries to answer the question *where do writers get their ideas?* that no writer seems to be able to answer with certainty, but when all is said and done she implies the same conclusion that I had come to long ago: we get our ideas from life and what C. G. Jung called our "transcendent function," which seems to be that aspect of our creative unconscious that Professor Harold Bloom contends to be the writer's personal *daimon.*

But perhaps this will become less abstruse in the course of this journal, which appears to be taking on a life of its own as the *daimonic* spirit of my writing life takes hold of me. To answer Siri's question *"why one story and not another?"* then, I have to reply that a writer's *daimon* has a mind of its own that chooses the story and its direction, and this is the mystery of creative writing that Norman Mailer called "spooky" and my high school hero and literary mentor has called me back to with my Christmas gift of an *Indigo Hemingway Notebook* from Penny's sister...

2. Coming Full Circle

I had to check out the magazine that the young journalist Aaron Hotchner worked for when he was sent to Cuba by his editor where "Papa" Hemingway lived to ask him if he would write a feature article on "The Future of Literature" (according to his first wife Hadley Richardson, Ernest got the affectionate nickname "Papa" when he was only twenty-six, in Pamplona, Spain where they had gone to see the running of the bulls and which may have come about because their son "Bumby" called him "Papa," but Hemingway loved being called "Papa" and later gave it gravitas by calling women that were special to him "Daughter," like Marlena Dietrich; but Hemingway lived life so fully that he grew old quickly), so I went to my Hemingway book shelves and took down Hotchner's book *Papa Hemingway*.

It was *Cosmopolitan* magazine, popularly known as *Cosmo*; but when I started reading *Papa Hemingway* again (for the third time, because I had read it the second time for my book *The Lion that Swallowed Hemingway*), I was pulled back to my high school years when I fell in love with Hemingway's romantic life and laconic style of writing; but I'll never know what my life would have been like had I heeded my call to writing instead of heeding a higher calling that Somerset Maugham's novel *The Razor's Edge* summoned me to when I read it in grade twelve and was so moved by it that I had to look for an answer to the meaning and purpose of life like Maugham's intrepid but no less romantic hero Larry Darrell.

But I didn't put writing aside altogether as I feverishly sought an answer to the haunting question of my life *"who am I?"* that the artist Paul Gaugin implied in his painting titled *"Where do we come from? What are we? Where are we going?"* I read with an insatiable appetite and wrote incessantly, but writing wasn't my first priority as I led everyone to believe; it was a false but honest front that I kept up to hide my private compulsion to find my true self. And now all these many years later I find it ironic that I should find myself coming full circle back to my high school hero and literary mentor, and I wonder if I will live long enough to do justice to my call back to creative writing…

I achieved what I came into this world to achieve and found my lost soul which I wrote about in *The Summoning of Noman*, so not realizing myself as a creative writer doesn't really bother me (I had a dream a few years ago of myself in a future life as a very precocious young writer, which suggested that in my current lifetime I'm doing all the spadework required to become a gifted writer in a future life, not unlike Ernest Hemingway who was born with a gift for writing); but all the same, it would be gratifying to write all those stories waiting to be written, like "The Sunworshipper," based upon my experience with an offshoot Christian solar cult teaching that did irreparable damage to my eyesight; "An Elephant in the Room," based upon my experience with a New Age religion that I lived for over thirty years which turned out to be a potpourri of purloined ancient teachings; and "We May be Tiny, But We're Not Small," a story based upon my harrowing experience with my self-published novel *What Would I Say Today If I Were to Die Tomorrow?* that so upset the people of my hometown that Penny and I had to relocate to Georgian Bay for peace of mind; but I just can't seem to write these stories because they're still so close to home that it pains me to think about them.

I have many stories bursting to be written, and I don't know if I'll have enough time left to write them all; but even if I don't, I have no regrets because I've written the books I was called to write to get my story on record, the last two books being the most satisfying: *Death, the Final Frontier* and *The Merciful Law of Divine Synchronicity,* which I call my twin soul books because I interrupted writing the latter to write the former.

But now I've been called back to creative writing by the unexpected gift of an *Indigo Hemingway Notebook* and three more affirming coincidences, to write stories drawing upon my own experiences to elucidate the mysteries of the secret way of life that I found with Gurdjieff's teaching which I lived with passionate commitment, stories like those in my book of short stories *Sparkles in the Mist* and my new story *"Hemingway's Forgotten Notebooks"* that I wrote shortly after receiving my *Indigo Hemingway Notebook* from Penny's sister and which I may use for the title of a new book of stories.

And speaking of titles, I learned something vital about creative writing when I wrote *Jesus Wears Dockers* and its sequel *St. Paul's Conceit.* (The former is published and on Amazon, but the latter is still waiting to be published.) Both novels had working titles, but they gave birth to their own title while they were being written; that's how I came to see that writing a novel is a sophisticated form of higher thinking that resolves karmic issues that have to be resolved so one can continue on one's journey to wholeness and completeness. That's how I came to see that a writer does not choose the books they write; rather, the books choose them because they *have* to be written so they can realize their own individuality, or what John Keats called "a bliss peculiar to each one by individual existence."

"There may be intelligences or sparks of divinity in millions," wrote Keats in a letter to his brother, "but they are not Souls till they acquire identities, till each one is personally itself." This, I was to learn after many years of living the imperative of the secret way of life, is the purpose of our existence—to realize our own individual identity, a separate "I" that can only be realized through the process of individuation through continuous life experience.

"How then are Souls to be made?" asks Keats. "How then are these sparks which are God to have identity given them—so as to possess a bliss peculiar to each one by individual existence? How but by the medium of a world like this?" But it took many years for me to see the wisdom of Keats's poetic genius, and only because I had the serendipitous experience of seven past-life regressions that revealed the sacred mystery of soul's individuation through life, an experience which I wrote about in my autobiographical novel *Cathedral of My Past Lives* (not yet published) and my memoir *Gurdjieff Was Wrong But His Teaching Works.*

This may be why I've been called back to creative writing, because I painfully learned while writing all of my books (especially my four volumes of spiritual musings) that the best way to reveal the sacred knowledge of the secret way of life is through poetry and literature. This is why people like Professor Bloom are so mystified

10

by poetry and literature that they cannot get enough of either, because poetry and literature *are* the secret way of life played out in the human condition, and by secret way of life I mean the natural process of realizing our own identity through the *enantiodromiac dynamic* of everyday experience.

This is why writers *have* to write. Creative writing initiates the writer into the mysterious individuation process of the secret way of life; but as virtually every writer sadly comes to see, writing is not enough to satisfy the longing in their soul for wholeness and completeness. This is what plagues Professor Bloom with "literary melancholia," the tragic realization that the way of poetry and literature is not enough to satisfy the archetypal longing in one's soul for wholeness and completeness; a very painful place to be.

"Whitman redefines the self, in which the self, the soul, and the real Me or Me Myself are three separate parts of the human entity, and his problem is how to reconcile and fuse the three, and he discovers that he cannot fuse them," said Professor Bloom in his interview with Paul Holdengraber at the NY Public Library, with tears in his tremulous voice. But I did. I found the secret way of life and took evolution into my own hands and realized my true self by fusing every aspect of myself into an individual self with what Gurdjieff called *"conscious effort"* and *"intentional suffering,"* thereby giving gnostic confirmation to the ancient alchemist saying: *"Man must finish the work which nature has left incomplete."*

This makes my story so unique that it borders on unbelievable, and I suspect I've been called back to creative writing so I can reflect the mystery of self-individuation through the integrative process of writing stories, the most effective way to explore the truth of the human condition that speaks to the enantiodromiac dynamic of our becoming…

3. The Daimon Knows How It Is Done

Saturday, March 4, 2017

The redoubtable literary critic and Yale Professor of Literature Harold Bloom wrote a new book called *The Daimon Knows* whose title he got from Ralph Waldo Emerson's essay "Self-Reliance," and I put this book on my Amazon wish list that my life partner Penny Lynn gave me for Christmas, along with Professor Bloom's *The Western Canon* and ten other books (the one I read first though was *Max Perkins, Editor of Genius,* because Maxwell Perkins nurtured and launched Hemingway's career by publishing his novel *The Sun Also Rises* which was inspired by Hemingway's life-changing experience in Pamplona, Spain), but what exactly did Emerson mean by saying that the *daimon* knows how it is done?

Is the *daimon* God within, as Emerson believed? Is it the Over-Soul, man's Higher Self? These are impossible questions to answer, but as Gurdjieff liked to say, *"There is only self-initiation into the mysteries of life,"* and many writers and artist will attest (maybe not openly) to some omniscient guiding force in their work; but I can't speak for anyone but myself, and my experience confirms what Emerson said in his essay "The Over-Soul" that "within man is the soul of the whole; the wise silence; the universal beauty, to which every part and particle is related; the eternal ONE."

I have no idea how Ralph Waldo Emerson came to this realization (I'd have to read everything he wrote and about him to find the answer, if it's there to be found), nor can I ever know how the young poet John Keats came to the realization that we are all sparks of God that come into this world to realize our own identity; but I do know that I had an experience which confirms both Emerson and Keats, an experience that inspired my novel *Cathedral of My Past Lives* which was based upon seven past-life regressions that I had the second year Penny and I relocated to Georgian Bay, Southcentral Ontario where we built our new home.

Ever since I read Jess Stearn's book *The Search for the Soul: The Psychic Lives of Taylor Caldwell* in my early twenties, I wanted to write a book on my own past lives, and when Penny and I moved to Georgian Bay serendipity introduced me to a past-life regressionist, and to my shock and wonder in my fourth regression I went all the way back to the Body of God where all souls come from; but I did not have a reflective self-consciousness. I was an embryonic soul immersed in the infinite love and bliss of God's Body (I *actually* experienced the ineffable joy of *just being*), but I had no self-consciousness; and in the same regression I went back to my first primordial human lifetime as an alpha male of a group of ten or twelve higher primates where I *actually* experienced the dawning of my own reflective self-consciousness that set me apart from my group for the rest of my life.

This was my experience, but it took more than ten years of compulsive writing to connect the dots and confirm that this was the primary archetypal pattern of every soul, that we all come from God as embryonic souls to evolve through life for the purpose of giving birth to a new "I" of God through the natural process of individuating our own identity just as Keats intuited in his letter to his brother; but not in one lifetime alone. It takes many incarnations to realize the identity of our essential nature, with each new life that we live adding to what Keats called "a bliss peculiar to each one by individual existence," and which eventually leads to what Jesus referred to in his secret teaching of the *way* as being born again to complete the process that nature cannot finish and become a new "I" of God.

"Verily, verily, I say unto thee," said Jesus to the Pharisee Nicodemus, *"except a man be born again, he cannot see the kingdom of God."* This spiritual rebirth is the essential purpose and meaning of life, which nature cannot complete for us; that's why Jesus brought the sacred teachings of the secret way of life into the world, to help souls find their way to wholeness and completeness. But this is difficult if not impossible to comprehend.

"That which is born of the flesh is flesh, and that which is born of the Spirit is spirit. Marvel not I said unto thee, Ye must be born again," said Jesus to Nicodemus, who was puzzled by how an old man could enter his mother's womb and be born again; but Jesus was referring to spiritual rebirth, which is the teleological purpose of

13

our existence; and not until one finds the secret way of life and lives it with conscious purpose and intention will one satisfy the longing in their soul for wholeness and completeness. This was my purpose, and my quest; and having experienced my rebirth one surprising summer day in my mother's kitchen while she was kneading bread dough on the kitchen table (after years of "working" on myself with *conscious effort* and *intentional suffering*), I acquired the sacred knowledge of the secret way of life, which I can neither prove nor disprove (or need to, for that matter), and this is what I've been called to write about in my stories; but I tremble at the thought. Which is why I keep putting off typing up the last two stories of *Sparkles in the Mist,* because they're so close to home that I cannot bring myself to re-experience those raw emotions.

And I procrastinate. Until the coincidences pile up again, like they did the other day with all those signs pointing me back to Hemingway who inspired me in high school to become a creative writer like him; but to my wonder, I was inflicted with an immortal wound in grade twelve when I read Maugham's novel *The Razor's Edge* that pierced my heart and set my soul on fire, and my life took a different turn. But I have no choice now but to heed my call back to creative writing or suffer the guilt of not being true to myself, which is a pain like no other.

"I can work in my garden all day long and enjoy it" said Nobel laureate Doris Lessing, "but if I miss one day of writing I regret it." That's the kind of guilt a writer feels when they're not being true to their calling, because their muse summons them to their *way,* their personal path to wholeness and completeness; and this is the inherent logic of the secret way of life that writers cannot fathom. But why?

The secret way of life is a sacred mystery, the inherently self-transcending process of individuation that will not reveal itself until one lives it consciously, which I did as I "worked" on myself with Gurdjieff's teaching, and the more dots that I connected as I lived the secret way of life, the more I saw through the mystery of creative writing that Norman Mailer called "spooky." And when I connected enough dots to see through the mystery, I saw that it was one's own *daimon* (the God within that knows how it is done) calling one to realize their true nature through the path they have been called to, like the way of creative writing that I have been called back to.

14

The *daimon* knows which story a writer has to write to satisfy the longing in their soul for wholeness and completeness, but this is so difficult to prove that only another writer would understand it; but because I trust my muse (God within, or what I prefer to call my "superior insight" like Carl Jung) I got confirmation for this insight, as I always do when I'm working on a new book, when serendipity verified it for me with another writer's experience.

I picked up my weekend papers yesterday, and in Saturday's *Globe and Mail* (*March 4, 2017*) I came upon an interview with the writer Emma Richler, the daughter of our famous Canadian novelist Mordecai Richler. The BOOK REPORT interview was captioned in bold letters: **"I never begin a book without a fierce compulsion."** I read the interview and was startled by Emma Richler's confirmation that a writer does not choose the books they write, they choose the writer.

"Why did you write your new book?" BOOK REPORT asked Emma Richler.

"Why? Why? Is this an existential question? Why write a book at all one might ask?" she replies. "Fey as it might sound, I think that the choosing of one story over another is a decision that is entirely out of the writer's hands. It is true of me, at any rate. Why this story, why at this time in my life, where do the characters come from, these themes, these obsessions? I am hard put to answer such questions, and they do not truly concern me. All I can swear to is that *I never begin a book without a fierce compulsion.* I have little doubt that the interest and obsessions lurk within from the earliest days and at a certain point in my writing life. Quite simply emerge as voices and faces in times and places, they begin to interact, they find expression. Now I begin a book, this particular book. It's not idle compulsion, no casual decision."

"What's more important: the beginning of a book, or the end?" she was asked.

"Both are hard, both are exciting, larger than the writer. I do not consider one more important than the other. *I do find that the end of a novel contains a germ or a hint of one's next beginning,* even if one only half knows it. So the end is a beginning, too. Every exit, an entrance," replied Emma Richler, with prescient insight into the mysterious process of the individuation process that creative writing realizes.

Emma Richler is not alone in her fierce compulsion to write a new story when she is called, because creative writing *is* the path that she was called to to complete what nature cannot finish, just as Siri Hustvedt said in her essay "Why One Story and Not Another?": "Every good novel has to be written. The need to tell it is compelling." And she further adds, "Once my characters have been born, they direct me. I have sometimes wanted to force them into situations, and they adamantly refuse." Once again, this is the "spooky" art of writing, the mysterious process of individuation impelled by the writer's *daimon*.

I've experienced this fierce compulsion many times in my writing life, sometimes so fiercely that I felt possessed almost beyond control (my *daimon* possessed me beyond my control once in high school when I sprang out of bed one morning and my poem "Noman" poured out of me like molten lava and which I did not decipher until fifty years later when I wrote *The Summoning of Noman*), so I have no problem understanding Emma Richler's compulsion to write; but there are writers who insist that they are in control of their story and their characters, like the popular novelist Richard Ford.

"My characters do what I want them to do," said Richard Ford, with that foolish arrogance that writers are prone to—until they admit to themselves that there really is something "spooky" about the creative process of writing, which seems to be an emerging theme of this journal on my writing life that my *daimon* is now directing...

4. Hemingway's Lust for Life

Tuesday, March 7, 2017

On the cover of my *Indigo Hemingway Notebook* that Penny's sister gave me for Christmas was written, capped in embossed golden letters, the great writer's credo: **IN ORDER TO WRITE ABOUT LIFE FIRST YOU MUST LIVE IT**.

This Ernest Hemingway did, not with normal human passion but with a voracious hunger to experience as much life as he could to satisfy the irrepressible longing in his soul for more personal identity and become the greatest writer of the 20th Century, and then he wrote about his experiences in his short stories and novels.

Hemingway was born with an adventurous spirit and travelled widely in his lust for life. He loved hunting wild game, especially big-game in Africa and Wyoming and Sun Valley, Idaho where he bought the house he died in, fishing trout streams, and especially deep-sea fishing on his boat *Pilar* in the Gulf Stream, drinking, which he did all of his life and curtailed only near the end for health reasons, eating, have sex, which he boasted about when drinking and in his letters (his last three marriages all began as affairs), boxing, which he did from an early age (he loved to shadow box with dead literary giants like Dostoevsky and Turgenev; his dream was to get into the ring with Tolstoy), bullfighting (he was an *affascinato* par excellence) and writing stories (all of his novels began as short stories), which gave him more satisfaction than any other passion because writing satisfied the longing in his soul more than any other passion, and this is the mystery of the secret way of life.

The archetypal pattern of every soul is to realize its own identity, as I creatively worked out from my past-life regressions that inspired my novel *Cathedral of My Past Lives*, and not until someone proves otherwise will I be dissuaded from this conviction which was born of my own individuation process that I precipitated by "working" on myself with conscious, willful intention; so when Hemingway said he loved writing more than any other passion in his life I understood what he meant, because writing was central to my own individuation process. But not as central as it was to Hemingway, because I had found the secret way and lived it with conscious, willful intention while Hemingway sought it through writing.

Writing was Hemingway's *way* to wholeness and completeness, his personal process of self-individuation that transmuted his life experiences into the self he longed to be; that's why he loved writing more than any other passion, including marlin fishing which was next to heaven for Hemingway. But because the longing in his soul was so great he had to experience all the life he could to process through writing for his own *becoming,* and he did everything possible to satisfy his passion for more life (he even played with androgynous love-making with his marriage partners, which he wrote about in his novel *The Garden of Eden*); that's why at the end of his life when he was treated at the Mayo clinic with electroshock therapy that affected his memory he became so dejected that he wanted to kill himself, because he could no longer write and had no reason left to live.

"It doesn't matter that I don't write for a day or a year or ten years as long as the knowledge that I can write is solid inside me. But a day without that knowledge, or not being sure of it, is eternity," he told his young friend Aaron Hotchner when he was being treated for depression and mental illness at the clinic; and he went on to say, "Hotch, if I can't exist on my own terms, then existence is impossible. Do you understand? That's how I've lived, and that's how I *must* live—or not live." But the great literary lion could no longer live on his own terms, and the second time he was released from the Mayo clinic he shot himself with his favorite double-barreled bird shotgun at his home in Ketchum, Idaho.

That's what inspired my book *The Lion that Swallowed Hemingway* three years ago. And now, for reasons which I'm working out in this journal of my writing life, I've been called back again to my high school hero and literary mentor...

When I was living in Annecy, France in 1968 where I had fled to get away from myself and begin my quest for my true self, I had a dream one night with the great Ernest "Papa" Hemingway. This would have been seven years after his suicide. He looked over my shoulder as I was writing at my desk, grizzled looking and menacing, and he said something that took me years to appreciate because I was much too culturally shocked and confused then. With a bluntness that surprised me, he said: *"I have pissed out more life than you have lived."*

I don't doubt Hemingway's comment now, forty-nine years later, knowing what I know from all the biographies that I've read on his life-packed life (my favourite is still *Papa Hemingway* for its insight into the great writer's private life a few years prior to winning the Nobel Prize in 1954 until his death in 1961, although I love the wickedly brilliant historical novel *The Paris Pilgrim* by Clancy Carlile that gives us a fictional account of Hemingway's early life like no biography possibly could), and if Hemingway were to repeat what he said in my dream, I'd happily say: "You probably did piss out more life than I had lived, but I achieved what I came into this world to achieve, and I have no regrets for my life."

I would say this not to be hurtful, because I know that he died with undying regret for betraying his wife Hadley by having an affair with Hadley's so-called friend Pauline Pfeiffer. "When I saw my wife again standing by the tracks as the train came in by the piled logs at the station, I wished I had died before I ever loved anyone but her," he wrote in his memoir *A Moveable Feast*; but then, Hemingway wouldn't be Hemingway had he not left Hadley for Pauline, and Pauline for Martha Gellhorn, and Martha Gellhorn for Mary Welsh.

Handsome, charming, talented, and mercilessly opportunistic Ernest Hemingway became a great writer because he was driven to be the best writer of his generation, never missing an opportunity to advance his career, and some would say that he is America's greatest writer and perhaps the greatest writer of the 20th Century; but whether he is or not does not matter to me, because Hemingway touched me in a way that no other writer has, and I continue to learn from his life and writing. But what is it that I have to learn now that I've been called back again to my high school hero and literary mentor?

The last time I was called back to Hemingway, serendipity introduced me to the movie *Hemingway and Gellhorn* playing on TV while Penny was setting the table for dinner. We had our neighbors over for dinner, but I *had* to watch the movie because Hemingway was my high school hero and literary mentor; so I set up a TV tray and watched the tempestuous relationship between Ernest Hemingway and his third wife Martha Gellhorn play out, and this movie gave me an insight into Hemingway's personality that set free the book inside me waiting to be written, my literary memoir *The Lion that Swallowed Hemingway.*

"How do you find a lion that has swallowed you?" asked C. G. Jung, the other hero in my personal memoir of self-discovery, and as I watched Hemingway's shadow-afflicted personality tango with his equally strong-willed wife Martha Gellhorn, I got the insight I needed to put the vital piece of the puzzle into place, and suddenly I saw through Hemingway and burst out, shocking Penny and our dinner guests, *"That's it! He had to have that to become a great writer! Hemingway had to be a prick to become the great writer that he became!"* The man and the writer became one person, and the mystery of his paradoxical personality made sense to me; that's why I *had* to write *The Lion that Swallowed Hemingway,* because the movie had set my insight free.

And that's what I mean when I say that writers don't choose the books they write; they choose the writer when he or she is ready to write them. And I wrote *The Lion that Swallowed Hemingway* with a compulsion equal to my need, and my need was great because I could not contain my insight into the *enantiodromiac* nature of man's paradoxical personality. But I had all the knowledge that I had acquired from Jung's psychology of individuation to guide me, and I wrote *The Lion that Swallowed Hemingway* in less than six weeks.

That was three years ago. Now I've been called back again to my high school hero and literary mentor, and I cannot help but wonder what my *daimon* wants of me...

5. Hemingway's Greatest Fear

Thursday, March 9, 2017

I let the fire burn out in our air-tight wood stove yesterday so I could clean the ashes out this morning, and then I lit a new fire, poured a fresh cup of coffee, added a shot of brandy and a teaspoon of honey, and read Hemingway's short story "Fathers and Sons" in front of the warm fire, and I came upon a line that I had highlighted the first time I read the story that jumped out at me again but with much more relevance this morning: "If he wrote it, he could get rid of it. He had gotten rid of a lot of things by writing them."

The story was about Hemingway's young self and his father, whom he loved and hated. *"That's it!"* I exclaimed again. *"That's why I've been called back to Hemingway! I have to work through my own issues by writing about them!"*

That's what Hemingway did with his Nick Adams stories, and all of his other stories and novels for that matter, because that was his way to wholeness and completeness; which was why Hemingway *had* to write every day with what Hotchner called a "monastic discipline," treating his writing like a sacred duty and holy ritual that he had to do every morning regardless how much he drank the night before, and he was a heavy drinker.

It was sacred because a writer's way is *their* path to wholeness and completeness, and nothing could be more sacred. I say this because I found the secret way of life and lived it with conscious, willful intention; and by secret way of life I mean soul's natural path to wholeness and completeness, whether one sees it or not.

But there's much more to my new call back to Hemingway, and I think I know what it is now because of something I had highlighted but which jumped out at me again with much more relevance yesterday morning while reading the concluding chapters of *Papa Hemingway,* something that revealed Hemingway's greatest fear.

Orest Stocco

"The worst death for anyone is to lose the center of his being, the thing he really is," said Hemingway to his young friend Hotchner. "Retirement is the filthiest word in the language. Whether by choice or by fate, to retire from what you do—and what you do makes you what you are—is to back up into the grave."

That's why Hemingway took his own life; he could no longer do what he loved and *had* to do, because writing transformed his life experience into the self he longed to be. In Professor Bloom's words, writing fused Hemingway's many aspects into his true self; which was why he was most himself when writing, and if he could not write he had no reason to live. That was the great writer's logic, which one could call selfish but which Hemingway would say was being true to himself. And that's the mystery of his paradoxical personality that I explored in *The Lion that Swallowed Hemingway*.

But I can't help but feel that there's another mystery waiting for me to resolve in my new call back to Hemingway, a mystery about my own nature which will only reveal itself when I work it out through the stories that I have avoided writing all these years because I was too caught up in my struggle to make a life for Penny and myself to write about my private life the way my high school hero and literary mentor did, my favorite Hemingway story being "The Snows of Kilimanjaro" because it bared his conflicted, tortured soul.

In the "Snows of Kilimanjaro" Hemingway's protagonist Harry betrayed his talent by squandering it, and he loathed himself for his self-betrayal; that's the core of his being that Hemingway was terrified of losing, and in "The Snows of Kilimanjaro" he played out in fiction what it would have been like to compromise himself and lose his core self like his fictional Harry did; that's why he *had* to write—because it kept him honest and true to himself. But Hemingway had a paradoxical personality, and as a man he faltered miserably.

"He's a pathological liar and the cruelest man I know," said his third wife Martha Gellhorn, even going so far as to call him an apocryphiar who believed his own lies, like his exaggerated war stories and other imagined conquests; and she had to leave him for her own peace of mind and budding career in journalism (the only one of his four wives to walk away from the great Ernest Hemingway),

22

because she could no longer suffer the vicious shadow side of his ego-inflated personality which came out in full when he was drinking.

But that was the man and not the writer who built every story that he wrote upon the integrity of "one true sentence." That's what made him bigger than life and a mythic figure who became one of the world's great literary legends. I loved the writer and grew to hate the man the more I got to know him, and then I saw the movie *Hemingway and Gellhorn* and everything that I had learned about the shadow side of the personality fell into place, and I was no longer mystified by the great writer's complex nature; and that, to my great relief, made me much less judgmental about Hemingway's paradoxical personality...

6. Our Goldfish "Goober"

Maybe, maybe not; but I think I'm beginning to sniff out the reason I was called to write this journal on my writing life, because with each book I write another piece of the puzzle falls into place and life makes much more sense to me, like the piece of the puzzle that fell into place when I wrote *The Lion that Swallowed Hemingway* with my insight into the *enantiodromiac* nature of man's paradoxical personality—i.e., the bifurcating dual consciousness of man's ego personality and repressed shadow self.

Instead of life making less sense to me, as is the case with so many writers who become more bewildered by life as they get older, life parts its veils a little more with every book I'm called to write, and I never cease to marvel at what I see.

But what, exactly, do I see that other writers can only catch a glimpse of—if they are lucky? Quoting Thomas Wolfe's alter ego in *You Can't Go Home Again*, I could simply say "The *way*! The *way*! Do you understand?" That's what I see; but what the hell does that mean, anyway? That's so metaphysical it's off-putting. And yet; and yet…

In my new call back to Hemingway (God, I hope this doesn't sound like a tired cliché), I felt compelled to re-read my books on Hemingway's life while delving again into his short stories and novels, but only this time I will be doing so with a fuller understanding of the legendary writer's complex nature which will add new texture to his life (I'm fascinated by how a writer turns his life into fiction), and the book I was called to re-read first was *Remembering Ernest Hemingway*, by James Plath and Frank Simons, with an insightful forward by Ernest Hemingway's granddaughter Lorian Hemingway (Hemingway's gender-conflicted second son Gregory's daughter); and this was immediately followed by *The True Gen: An Intimate Portrait of Hemingway By Those Who Knew Him,* by the biographer and novelist Denis Brian. Both books proved more enlightening in my second reading.

But before I go any further in this journal of my writing life, it's only fair to confess that despite the impression I may have given I've yet to read all of Hemingway's books. I haven't read his posthumous novels *The Garden of Eden* and *True at First Light,* and neither have I read *Death in the Afternoon* and some of his short stories that I kept putting off for one reason or another. Shameless, but true. But why haven't I read them, given that Hemingway had and continues to have such a powerful influence upon my writing life?

The most honest answer that I can offer, after exhausting all legitimate and illegitimate excuses, is that Hemingway's personal life as a *daimonically* driven writer fascinated me more than his writing— because his life was so damn romantic and alluring!

Hemingway had the temerity to live the life he wanted to live, and no one was going to get in his way to keep him from living it— not his domineering mother who disapproved of his life, his henpecked father who initiated him into the exciting world of trout fishing and hunting, good and loyal writer friends that he used and betrayed, loving and bitter wives or anybody else—Ernest Hemingway got what Ernest Hemingway wanted, whatever the cost; and then he wrote about his life with the objectivity of a true artist. As he said in *By-Line: Ernest Hemingway:* "The more he (a writer) learns from experience, the more truly he can imagine it," and Hemingway "imagined" his life into some of the world's best literature.

There, I've gotten that skunk off my conscience. Perhaps, then, I have begun to do what my new call back to Hemingway impels me to do—exorcise some of my own demons through writing, demons born of my own inauthenticity, the same kind of demons that plagued my high school hero and literary mentor all of his life and which accounted for the paradoxically nature of his irresolvable authentic/inauthentic personality, the only difference being that I resolved myself enough to *become* my true self and Hemingway didn't.

That's what I explored in my literary memoir *The Lion that Swallowed Hemingway.* But it seems that my new call back to Hemingway wants me to dig deeper into his life and mine so I can grow more fully in a larger paradigm of personal meaning which, coincidentally enough, was confirmed yesterday by the symbolic message of our goldfish "Goober."

The Oracle of Life is always speaking to us in signs and symbols, and the Oracle of Life spoke to me yesterday through Penny's suggestion that we get a new tank for our goldfish Goober because he had grown too big for his tank and swam in a curled-up manner that concerned us; so she came home from work yesterday with a larger tank which we set up immediately, but he still swam with his body curved into a circle.

"Give him a day or two," I said, with an intuitive feeling that he had to adjust to his new and larger "paradigm of meaning," and which he did because this morning he began swimming as he normally did before "outgrowing" his tank.

This is a metaphor, of course; but that's how the Oracle of Life speaks to us—in signs and symbols that speak to our situation; and if we are conscious enough to "see" and "hear" what the Oracle of Life is trying to tell us, we can take the message and continue on our journey through life with much more mobility and personal freedom.

So it seems that the Oracle of Life was just confirming with our goldfish Goober and his larger tank the reason I was called back to Hemingway, because I need more space; meaning, I need to expand my paradigm of personal meaning by resolving aspects of myself that inhibit my growth as a writer, and by re-exploring Hemingway and writing the stories that I keep putting off I will be doing just that, and I honestly believe this message because I trust the Oracle of Life implicitly. And today I'm going to finish reading *The True Gen* and one or two of Hemingway's stories that I haven't read yet...

7. A Literary Message from "Goober"

Thursday, March 16, 2017

To explain, several months ago we noticed Goober swimming with his tail curled and almost touching his head and we thought he was just diverting himself; but then he began to concern Penny, and several times she felt he was dying, but he didn't.

"He's grown too big for his tank, that's why he's swimming like that," I said to Penny, intuiting the reason for his contorted body which had now become his new normal; but Goober didn't look right, like he had curled in upon himself, and he began to worry us.

"Should we get him a larger tank?" Penny, who curiously enough suffocated in her seventeen-year marriage before we met and fell in love, finally asked me.

"We could, but he's so old he could croak anytime," I said, and we put off getting a larger tank until the other day when Penny called from Walmart in Wasaga Beach to tell me that she was going to buy a new tank for Goober.

And now Goober is swimming straight and normal, which didn't surprise me because he has much more space to stretch his body and swim more freely, just as Penny felt more free in our relationship, and that's when I heard the silent voice of the Oracle of Life speaking to me…

I *knew* I had been called back again to Hemingway when Penny's sister gave me an *Indigo Hemingway Notebook* for Christmas, and I dove right in and wrote a story called "Hemingway's Forgotten Notebooks" (Hemingway wrote *A Moveable Feast* based upon his Parisian notebooks that he found in a steamer trunk that he had stored away in the basement of the Ritz Hotel in Paris and forgotten about for years), but I couldn't quite reconcile my feelings about being called back again to my high school hero and literary mentor.

Was I afraid to explore my life creatively like Hemingway did in his Nick Adams stories and all of his other stories and novels? This wasn't the first time I was called back to writing stories. Two years ago I had a dream that inspired my book *Enantiodromia and Other Stories,* but after writing ten stories I stopped working on the book because I couldn't bring myself to write the final story based upon my experience of a dear friend's death by cancer, and I moved on to edit my novel *An Atheist, An Agnostic, and Me* that I had written fifteen years earlier; but I wasn't more than a third of the way through when I got called to write *The Merciful Law of Divine Synchronicity* which got interrupted while writing chapter twelve when I was called to write *Death, the Final Frontier*, and when I finished writing this book I finished writing *The Merciful Law of Divine Synchronicity,* and then I was called back to Hemingway; but why? Why was I called back to writing stories? *Why why why?*

That's what the Oracle of Life symbolically revealed to me with Goober and his larger tank, telling me that by writing the stories I've been avoiding all of these years I will expand my literary horizons and paradigm of personal meaning, like Hemingway did with every new story that he wrote. "Do not worry. You have always written before and you will write now. All you have to do is write one true sentence," He wrote in *A Moveable Feast,* the memoir of his apprenticeship years in Paris, and he worked with such passionate commitment on his stories that he would become an inspiration for countless young writers like myself (young Mordecai Richler went to Paris also, as did the short story writer Mavis Gallant who ended up making Paris her home for the rest of her life); but after writing *The Lion that Swallowed Hemingway*, why was I called back again to Hemingway with the Christmas gift of an *Indigo Hemingway Notebook* and the message from our goldfish Goober?

I have no doubt that after receiving my *Hemingway Notebook* that called me back to Hemingway that the Oracle of Life was confirming the message with Goober and his new tank, and I knew that if I failed to heed the message I would inhibit my growth as a creative writer; that's why I had to read Hemingway in full this time, because I knew that the deepest truths of a writer's life could only be found in the stories he wrote and not in biographies and memoirs— just as our own short story writer and winner of the Nobel Prize for

Literature Alice Munroe said to Shelagh Rogers in a CBC interview: *"Memoir is the facts of life. Fiction is the truth of life."* And I believe that what Hemingway has to teach me this time around is to muster my courage and write the stories I've been putting off writing, because that's how I can resolve the deeper issues of my life and grow as a person and creative writer.

That's the literary message I got from Goober, because *the universal truths of life are found in the individual human experience,* something that my high school hero and literary mentor knew intuitively. "Nobody really knows or understands and nobody has ever said the secret. The secret is that it is poetry written into prose and it is the hardest of all things to do," said Hemingway to his wife Mary in her memoir *How It Was*; and because it's so hard to do, I keep putting off writing the stories that the Oracle of life keeps calling me back to write.

But I can take my cue from a letter that Hemingway wrote to his friend F. Scott Fitzgerald (who introduced him to his publisher Maxwell Perkins). Fitzgerald had fallen into a slump, and Hemingway wrote: "Forget your personal tragedy. We are all bitched from the start and you especially have to be hurt like hell before you can write seriously. But when you get the damn hurt use it—don't cheat with it. Be as faithful to it as a scientist—but don't think anything is of any importance because it happens to you or anyone belonging to you."

Hemingway paid a dear price with every story that he wrote, but he also gained in the writing because it kept him honest; but when he could no longer write because of his "black-ass" depression and mental breakdown, he killed himself. A tragic ending, but not surprising given the adventurous, alcohol-soaked life that he lived; but because he had the courage to write stories drawn from his own conflicted and tortured life, he gave us a glimpse of the secret that is poetry written into prose, and that's what I hope to do with my own stories that my *daimon* beckons me to write with my new call back to Ernest "Papa" Hemingway…

8. Hemingway's Secret

Friday, March 31, 2017

Some writers have it and some don't, the secret that is poetry written into prose; and Hemingway had it intuitively from the start of his writing career. I didn't have it, and I envied Hemingway. Not that I understood why I envied him, but I do now.

Was that why I kept putting off reading the rest of his stories and novels, because I resented his natural talent that he nurtured and developed with a passion that made me envious because I could not dedicate myself to writing like he did?

I was inflicted with an immortal wound when I read Maugham's novel *The Razor's Edge* in grade twelve, and I was compelled to find my real self; that's where my passion went. I could only spare so much time to reading literature, I had to make a living and seek out books that would help me find my real self, books that took me deeper into the sacred knowledge of the *way*, little realizing that the *way* was hidden in the depths of the human condition which gifted writers like Hemingway creatively mined in their writing.

That's the irony of my life, that I could have pursued creative writing; but I didn't. I had to go where I was called, and I was called to the higher path of looking for my real self which transcended all other paths because all other paths only make one ready for the *way*, like Katherine Mansfield who was called when she realized that literature was not enough to satisfy the longing in her soul and went to Gurdjieff to help her find her real self.

But that's why Hemingway *had* to write every day. His writing was his personal path to the *way*, which he intuited in the depths of the human condition. He had no idea that the secret way was life itself, but his call to writing pulled him deeper into the human condition through life experience; that's why he lusted for more and more life, because the more life he experienced, the closer he got to the secret that is poetry which he wrote into prose in stories like "The Short Happy Life of Francis Macomber." That's why his friend and poet Archibald MacLeish said to Denis Brian in *The True Gen* that Hemingway "was one of the most human and spiritually powerful creatures I have ever known."

All great writers live their life with all the passion of their *daimonic* need (the greater the need, the greater the writer; or so it seems), because they know intuitively that the passionate life makes for great literature—or art, as the case may be. That's what the Hemingway quote on the cover of my *Indigo Hemingway Notebook* points to: **IN ORDER TO WRITE ABOUT LIFE FIRST YOU MUST LIVE IT**. That was his credo.

Hemingway ridiculed me with his comment in my dream in Annecy, France because he knew the secret way of life intuitively. *"I have pissed out more life than you have lived,"* he said to me, telling me in his own crude way that the secret that is poetry lies in the human experience, and the more one experiences life the closer they will get to the secret of life which, ironically, is the *way* that I found in my quest for my real self when serendipity introduced me to Gurdjieff's teaching while studying philosophy at university.

But I didn't know then that all roads led to Rome, so I was no less true to my calling than Hemingway was to his; but he didn't know that in my dream, did he? Hemingway ferreted out the secret way with his gift for writing, but I set out to look for the *way*, which made my quest more serious; and because I *lived* the secret that is poetry, I resolved the paradoxical nature of my personality and completed what nature could not finish. Hemingway didn't. His dark shadow side overpowered his ego personality, and he killed himself; but some of the stories that he wrote gave us a powerful insight into the secret that is poetry, like his story "A Clean, Well-Lighted Place" that speaks to the shadow side of human nature.

This is why I've been called back to Hemingway again, so I can write the stories that I keep putting off. I can write them with a conscious awareness of the secret way, which will give my stories an irony that would be much more beguiling than Hemingway's ice-berg theory that he made famous in *The Sun Also Rises* by not revealing the sexual dynamic between his hero Jake Barnes and the alluring Lady Brett Ashley, a literary technique that he discovered in his apprenticeship years in Paris while studying Cezanne's paintings in the Louvre. "I was learning something from the paintings of Cezanne that made writing simple true sentences far from enough to make the stories have the dimension that I was trying to put into them," wrote Hemingway in *A Moveable Feast*. "I was learning very much from him but I was not articulate enough to explain it to anyone. Besides it was a secret."

The secret that Hemingway intuited, I discovered consciously; which is why it took so many years to make sense of my feelings for my high school hero and literary mentor, because he had what I wanted, and I envied him. But that was then, and this is now; and in my new call back to Hemingway I can do him proper justice by reading the rest of his stories and novels to see how he used his life in his fiction, which I hope will inspire me to delve deeper into my own life and do the same. That's the *daimonic* drive of this journal...

9. The Professor's Dilemma

Saturday, April 1, 2017

Last Sunday morning I stepped out onto our front deck to get my paper that lay alongside our car in the driveway. It had rained in the night, but I hadn't noticed that the rain had turned to ice, and as I was about to step down the steps to fetch my paper I slipped on the glistening ice on the edge of our covered deck which I thought was water and landed on my backside and slid down the three steps and onto our driveway, banging the back of my head on one of the steps. I didn't quite see stars, but I felt the pain both in my head and my back, and I panicked instantly at what I might've done. *"Oh God,"* I said.

I didn't move. I didn't want to move. I just lay in grimacing pain as thoughts of a broken disk possessed me. I felt the back of my head again and didn't feel any lump forming, and then I put my hand to my back where it hurt most and just held it there trying to compose myself. Penny was still asleep and would never have heard me if I called, so I had to see if I could stand up on my own, which I finally managed to do, but I winced in great pain.

My slipper had flown from my right foot when I slipped and fell and landed ten or so feet away, close to my Sunday paper (*The Toronto Star, Sunday, March 26, 2017*), and very carefully I crippled my way to my slipper and paper, picking up my slipper first and then my paper, and walked very carefully on the black ice of our asphalt driveway and on up to the deck, holding onto the hand railing, and into the house and to the sun room where I carefully lowered my body into my recliner and stretched out as far as I could and lay there hoping to God that I hadn't done serious damage to my aching body.

I hadn't, but all week I've been sitting in my recliner in our sun room re-reading Professor Bloom's *The Western Canon* or watching TV with my electric heating pad soothing the muscles in my lower back, and in my writing room I sat in my reading chair with my heating pad switched on high while I watched videos of Professor Bloom interviews on *Charlie Rose* or listened to him interviewed on

Open Source Radio with the knowledgeable and insightful Christopher Lydon, and I also watched three seasons of the TV British court drama *Silk* as well as the complete series of the Belfast strangler called *The Wall,* and the complete Scottish crime drama called *Shetland.* My heating pad did wonders for my back!

I'm simply in awe of Professor Bloom's labyrinthine mind, and I marvel at how he connects the dots in literature and recites poetry at will; but I honestly feel sorry for him, and I wrote a poem to capture my feelings. I wrote this poem a few months ago, but if anything watching and listening to him again only re-enforced my feelings: —

The Professor's Dilemma

What does it matter if we die alone in a back
alley or at home in bed, death is an equal
opportunity provider; but life goes on, and no
one knows any better. So you have a scandalous
memory, preternatural reading skills, and more
literary knowledge than you know what to do
with, and still you flounder in ignorance of self
and meaning. I knew Keats too, and his vision
of the world; but as close as he came to God,
he too died unresolved. A cold eye, judgment,
the dreaded axe falls and chops the poet's head
off with the meanest truth: Sterling Professor
of the Humanities, seeker of Gnostic Wisdom,
what is it that you are looking for that the
gods of literature cannot satisfy?

I only have a few more chapters to read of *The Western Canon,* and in all honesty this second reading has been much more rewarding; but after listening to him in all those YouTube interviews talking about poets and novelists I can't help but feel that the great literary critic is trapped in the labyrinth of his own mind, which doesn't mean that he isn't a joy to listen to and read. That's why I've put three more of his books on my Amazon wish list: *How to Read and Why, The Anatomy of Influence,* and *The Best Poems of the*

English Language. Professor Bloom has an uncanny gift for seeing the archetypal spirit of literature at work in every writer (he had a powerful dream of a suffocating angel in his thirties that inspired his critical book *The Anxiety of Influence* which changed the course of literary criticism), but as to why I feel he's trapped in his own mind, I'll get into another time…

I was supposed to meet my niece from Oakville at *Moxie's Restaurant* in Barrie for lunch on Thursday, but I wasn't sure I could make it because I was still stiff and sore; but she called Thursday morning and cancelled because it called for freezing rain and she didn't want to risk driving, and I told her of my fall and she told me of the fall that my brother's wife in Thunder Bay had which landed her in the hospital. She slipped on ice too, but her fall broke her ankle and she had to have surgery and two pins installed. She's still in the hospital, and I thank my lucky stars that I've only got a sore back because it could have been serious.

We rescheduled our lunch for next Thursday, which we're both looking forward to because we haven't seen each other since our last meet-up at *Moxie's* last summer; my niece is the only member of my family that I talk to, but that would take a whole novel to explain if I could ever muster the courage to write it. Even Hemingway couldn't do it.

Hemingway used his whole life in his stories and novels, but he was careful when he wrote about his parents and siblings. His Nick Adams stories are drawn from his youth, stories like "Up in Michigan," "Big Two-Hearted River," and "Father's and Sons," but like all good writers he used his family's traits as he composed some of his fictional characters to give them what they needed to portray them with authenticity, like the artist Thomas Hudson and his three sons in Hemingway's posthumous novel *Islands in the Stream* that were modeled on himself and his three sons, Jack, Patrick and Gregory. Hemingway was merciless in his aesthetic for authenticity, especially with his gender-conflicted son Gregory.

"Good writing is true writing. If a man is making a story up it will be true in proportion to the amount of knowledge of life that he has and how conscientious he is; so that when he makes something up it is as it would truly be," said Hemingway in a collection of his journalism writing, *By-Line: Ernest Hemingway*. So I believe Saul Bellow's son Greg when he said, "If you want to know the truth about my father, read his novels. It's all there." As Alice Munro said, *"Memoir is the facts of life. Fiction is the truth of life."*

A writer bares his soul in his fiction, as Hemingway certainly did; especially in his critical failure, *Across the River and into the Trees*. Hemingway's foolish infatuation with a young Venetian girl may have made for great literature (he believed this was the best book he had ever written), and whether it is great literature or not still remains to be seen (I hated this novel), though the critics lambasted it; but he did bounce back with *The Old Man and the Sea* two years later which garnered him a Pulitzer and the Nobel Prize for Literature— "For his powerful, style-forming mastery of the art of modern narration, as most recently evinced in "The Old Man and the Sea." But then began Hemingway's breakdown and suicide.

I hope to read the rest of Hemingway's work in the next month or so while pursuing my own writing (I may begin a sequel to *Healing with Padre Pio* this summer), and I've been given a call through one of Penny's dreams to polish my novel *An Atheist, An Agnostic, and Me*, as well as edit and tighten my book of short stories *Sparkles in the Mist*; so, I have a busy schedule ahead of me, not to mention that I also promised to paint our house this summer. I hope I can see all of this through, but what will be will be...

10. The Labyrinth of Literature

Thursday, April 6, 2017

Like all life sayings, this one was also born of personal experience, and whether it holds any truth for others, it is certainly true for me: *If there's one thing we can be certain about life, it's that people will always disappoint you.* This has to be the meanest saying of my lifelong experience, but I stand by it…

It's been a hard couple of weeks. My back is still sore from my fall, and it hurts like hell whenever I cough or sneeze, and three days ago we learned that our tenant is moving out of the middle apartment of our triplex unit up north, which has thrown us into a mild confusion because we need the rental income; but we've been through this before, and we'll manage as we always do; and as I often do, I wrote a poem to capture the raw emotions:

Liquid Plumber

Give me cause to take a drink,
oh what a drunk I could have been;
another blow, another disappointment,
another change is in the air, —

Panic, and fear pours into my weary soul
like scalding liquid plumber, cleansing me
of all security and giving me cause
to drink and become a drunk.

The pastures are greener on the other side,
but fear blinds me; I pray and pray and pray
that it will go away, but life is here to stay,
here to stay, here to stay, here to stay, —

Oh what I drunk I could have been!

I also learned about swim bladder disease last week from Penny who went online to do some research on goldfish, which throws new light onto our goldfish Goober's message; but I will explore this later. For now, I want to say something about creative writing that was inspired by Professor Bloom's book *The Daimon Knows* that I started to read again after I finished re-reading *The Western Canon.*

The labyrinth of literature is vast and deep and ever-expanding, and Professor Bloom is the only person I know of who has the genius to explore it so freely with a brilliance that dazzles me, and in all honesty I cannot understand why the Nobel Prize continues to elude him. If they can award the Nobel Prize for Literature to the singer/songwriter Bob Dylan (2016), they certainly can award it to a man who has done more for literature than anyone with over forty books of literary studies to his credit, not including hundreds of volumes in *Bloom's Modern Critical Views* series. A colossal accomplishment.

Professor Bloom opened a window onto literature like no other literary scholar, or any writer for that matter; and even though he could not crack the code of the secret way of life implicit to literature, he has come closer than anyone; and that's the point I want to make with this journal on my writing life, because I cracked the code of the secret way of life.

Penny and I are proof-reading my book *The Merciful Law of Divine Synchronicity,* and this morning I read two more chapters, "The Wisdom of Literature," and "The Naked Truth Unveiled," and proofing these chapters brought to mind Professor Bloom's dilemma of not having found the resolution for what he perceived to be the archetypal purpose of literature, which C. G. Jung called the "process of individuation." This is why Professor Bloom cannot extricate himself from what he calls a "breathtaking kind of nihilism," which he believed was best expressed by William Shakespeare, followed by Walt Whitman, "an American, one of the roughs, a kosmos who could not reconcile his soul and his true self and so took up the middle ground between them"—which seems to be the most that literature can do for us.

What then is the inherent logic of literature that Professor Bloom cannot crack and is responsible for that breathtaking kind of nihilism that despairs him?

"Literature is not enough," said Katherine Mansfield to her literary mentor and editor Alfred R. Orage while living at Gurdjieff's Institute for the Harmonious Development of Man in Fontainebleau, France where she had gone to find her real self, and literature is not enough because it cannot resolve the paradox of man's dual nature— what Gurdjieff called our *essence* and *personality* and philosophers refers to as our *being* and *non-being*.

"Man must complete what nature cannot finish," said the ancient alchemists, and completing what nature cannot finish was what I was called to do in my quest for my true self; but why cannot nature finish what it started?

This haunts Professor Bloom and the reason that he remains stuck in the labyrinth of literature, because literature cannot provide the means to resolve the paradox of our inner and outer self so we can transcend ourselves, which is the only exit out of that breathtaking nihilism that literature has given birth to and continues to perpetuate with every new work.

And yet, ironically, literature does point to the way out of the labyrinth of life; this is why Professor Bloom said to Paul Holdengraber in an interview at the NY Public Library for his book *The Anatomy of Influence,* "criticism is the art of learning the hidden paths that lead from poem to poem," which brought to mind what Jung wrote in his commentary to Richard Wilhelm's translation of the ancient Taoist text *The Secret of the Golden Flower*: "…when I began my life-work in the practice of psychiatry and psychotherapy, I was completely ignorant of Chinese philosophy, and only later did my professional experience show me that in my technique I had been unconsciously led along the secret way which has been the preoccupation of the best minds of the East for centuries."

The "hidden paths that lead from poem to poem" are the secret way of life that Jung discovered, which is why he wrote in *The Red Book*, the remarkable record of his "confrontation with the unconscious": *"This life is the way, the long sought-after way to the unfathomable, which we call divine. There is no other way, all other ways are false paths."* So despite Professor Bloom's intuitive awareness of the "hidden paths that lead from poem to poem," he never managed to grab hold of the secret way that is the archetypal imperative of life and literature, and by this I mean man's instinctive impulse to self-reconciliation that cannot be completed by nature. To do this, man must live the secret way consciously.

This is why I was called to keep this journal on my writing life, because I *know* that all the hidden paths that lead from poem to poem will take one to the secret way, which if one can grasp and live it consciously like Emily Dickinson and Rumi they will complete what nature cannot finish and free themselves from the labyrinth of life and literature…

11. Hemingway's Call to Writing

Saturday, April 8, 2017

"You have to take what is not palpable and make it completely palpable and also have it seem normal and so that it can become a part of the experience of the person who reads it," said my high school hero and literary mentor in a letter to Bernard Berenson (1954), which Hemingway did with consummate skill; but writing meant much more to him than crafting a good story. Writing was his "hidden path" to the secret way which he sought with ever story that he wrote; that's what drove Hemingway to write every day.

In *The Paris Review* (Spring, 1958) George Plimpton asked Hemingway, "Can you recall an exact moment when you decided to become a writer?" And Hemingway replied, "No, I always wanted to be a writer." Which means quite simply that he was called to writing. But why? Why writing and not medicine like his father? Or music like his mother? Why is one called to one path and not another? That's the mystery of our *becoming…*

I heard the call to writing in elementary school, and in high school I fell in love with the romantic idea of being a writer like Ernest Hemingway; but then I was struck by an immortal wound when I read Somerset Maugham's novel *The Razor's Edge* and was called to become a seeker like Maugham's intrepid hero Larry Darrell, and my call to writing waned.

But I never stopped writing, I just poured most of my energies into my contract painting business that I started after leaving university and seeking answers to the imponderable question of my life, *who am I?* And I read voraciously, which took up a great deal of my time, books that had to do with my search for the way to my true self, many of which I ordered by mail from *Samuel Weiser Books* in New York City because I couldn't get them anywhere else, which included most of my books on Gurdjieff and his teaching.

I was always browsing the Philosophy, Religion, and New Age sections of book stores, and over time I accumulated a library of thousands of books; but after I found the answer to the imponderable question of my life I was pulled back to literature, because my quest for my true self had awakened me to the secret way that is the archetypal imperative that drives all writers to write; and in the poems and stories that they wrote I began to see the secret way of the writer's *way*, which heightened my appreciation for literature. That's why I was called back to my high school hero and literary mentor, because his passion for writing was so great that it destroyed him. *And that's the irony of Hemingway's life!*

In a letter to Ivan Kashkin (1935), Hemingway wrote: "…writing is something that you can never do as well as it can be done. It is a perpetual challenge and it is more difficult than anything else that I have ever done—so I do it. And it makes me happy when I do it well," which was well enough to garner him the most coveted prize in literature "for his powerful, style-forming mastery of the art of modern fiction."

Considering his daunting prowess for fishing (especially deep-sea fishing which inspired *The Old Man and the Sea*), hunting (which inspired *Green Hills of Africa* and two of his most canonical short stories, "The Short Happy Life of Francis Macomber" and "The Snows of Kilimanjaro"), and his intimate knowledge of bullfighting (which inspired *The Sun Also Rises*, *Death in the Afternoon,* and *A Dangerous Summer),* not to mention boxing which he loved to do (he was always shadow boxing with great writers) and which inspired his story "The Killers" that was made into a movie as were many of his short stories, but of all his passions—he loved sex enough to destroy his marriage to his first wife Hadley Richardson, the great love of his life (it was more complicated than that, but that went with his voracious need to be the greatest writer of his generation and his lover Pauline Pfeiffer fed his egoic need more than Hadley could as he worked on his breakaway novel *The Sun also Rises*), Ernest "Papa" Hemingway loved writing most of all; that's why he continues to fascinate me.

My fascination is not for his writing style alone, which I could never emulate no matter how hard I tried, but for being the man that he was—a man who lived his life with enough passion to satisfy ten lifetimes but not enough to satisfy the longing in his soul that inevitably drove him to despair and suicide; that's why I wrote *The Lion that Swallowed Hemingway.* But I've been called back to Hemingway once more, and I have to wonder why…

Yesterday I felt a strong desire to listen to Professor Bloom again (I can't get enough of his encyclopedic knowledge of literature), so I went on YouTube and listened to his interview again with Paul Holdengraber, then Eleanor Wachtel's interview on CBC's *Writers & Company* and Charlie Rose's interview on his book *Hamlet: Poem Unlimited,* and I learned that Shakespeare employed an amazing twenty-one thousand words to draw out the people in his plays. So uncannily did he draw them out that critics have said that his characters are more human than real people, which may give credence to Plato's theory of ideal forms, as though Shakespeare had ensouled his characters with their archetypal ideal, an unparalleled genius that inspired one of Professor Bloom's most insightful books, *Shakespeare: The Invention of the Human.* And finally, I listened once more to the *Arts Tonight* interview, "Portrait of a Literary Critic," and Professor Bloom brought me to tears with the despair in his voice because literature could not resolve the paradox of life, the dual consciousness of our inner and outer self. Here's Professor Bloom in his own voice:

"I think that ultimately the elliptical burden of what he (Shakespeare) gives us is a breathtaking kind of nihilism more uncanny than anything that Nietzsche apprehended. I think in the end he, among so much else, (is) telling us that there are no values, or value except those that we create or imbue events, people, things with. Emerson beautifully said, 'No world. There is no next world. Here and now is the whole fact.' And I think Hamlet understands that very well indeed that here and now is the whole fact; or that beautiful phrase, is it a Victor Hugo or Walter Pater, 'We have an interval and then our place knows us no more.' But that I think is what the highest literature is finally about. I tell my students that appreciation is what our stance towards the highest imaginative literature should be, and that what we have to appreciate are the only values that matter in the highest literature which are cognitive and aesthetic values quite apart from societal and even historical considerations. Immanuel Kant says that time and space are indeed appearances and are therefore in a sense illusory, but nevertheless he says there is something numinal, there is something permanent in those appearances, and I think you don't need Kant if you have Shakespeare. Of course Hamlet, among so much else, is telling you that. Our yearning at least is transcendental..."

The only hope that Professor Bloom sees in our longing to be whole is a transcendental yearning that literature cannot satisfy, which is why Shakespeare's Falstaff's love of life moves Professor Bloom more than any other character in all of literature.

"Give me more life," says the good Professor, like Falstaff; but it doesn't matter how much life one lives, it will never be enough to satisfy the longing in one's soul, as Hemingway knew only too well despite his great passion for life; but why? Why is life not enough to satisfy the longing in our soul for what Jung called "wholeness and completeness"? Why is life, and by consequence literature, not enough to satisfy our transcendental yearning?

This is the mystery of life, and literature…

12. The Style and the Man

Sunday, April 9, 2017

In a moment of unguarded candor, "Papa" confessed to his young friend "Hotch" that what they called his famous style came about because he was always awkward and inarticulate, and then one day he discovered "cablese" when submitting his journalism pieces from Europe to his editor at the Toronto *Star* (for economic reasons, he had to use the least number of words in his cables), and with the writing tips that he picked from the *Kansas City Star*'s 101 rules that governed the *Star*'s simple prose where he began his career in journalism, Hemingway cultivated his famous laconic style of writing, and studies have shown that his writing vocabulary consisted of only 900 words compared to Shakespeare's 21000.

William Faulkner, whom Hemingway bitterly resented because he got the Nobel Prize in 1949, five years before Hemingway got his in 1954, accused Hemingway of being afraid to use big words. "Poor Faulkner," Hemingway said to Hotchner in *Papa Hemingway.* "Does he really think big emotions come from big words? He thinks I don't know the ten-dollar words. I know them alright. But there are older and simpler and better words and those are the ones I use." That's what made Hemingway's simple style legendary.

More has been written about Hemingway's life and writing than most writers in the world, but all that interests me is what I can still learn from him; and to do that I have to read all of Hemingway's works so I can get a better feel of the man, because Hemingway's life can be found in his fiction, and Hemingway's life continues to fascinate me…

Hemingway was obsessed with truth in his writing. "The most essential gift for a good writer is a built-in, shockproof, shit detector. This is the writer's radar and all great writers have had it," he said to George Plimpton in *The Paris Review,* which is why he began every story that he wrote with "one true sentence" upon which he built the rest of his story, and that's where Hemingway's curse began, because the more successful and world famous he became, the more his ego grew and fed the false shadow side of his personality.

Hemingway was a complicated man, as all of his wives and friends knew, his literary imperative to be true to his art and his false shadow self possessing him, especially when drinking, and the conflict of his dual nature would pull him down into deep depression until he fell into such despair that he finally took his own life to free himself from himself; and it's this tragic dynamic of man's conflicted nature that pervades all of literature which Professor Bloom identified in Shakespeare as a "breathtaking kind of nihilism more uncanny than anything Nietzsche apprehended," a nihilism with "no exit," as Sartre concluded.

I read Sartre at university where I had gone to study philosophy in my quest for an answer to the imponderable question of my life, *who am I?* But as much as I admired and respected the brilliant dialectician for his intellectual integrity, I could not embrace his nihilistic philosophy; it was much too oppressive and depressing.

"Man is condemned to be free," said Sartre, like Professor Bloom who concluded that Shakespeare's burden of breathtaking nihilism confirmed that there are no values in life except those that we "create or imbue events, people, things with," but I just could not buy into this soul-crushing nihilism, regardless how sublime the poetic imagery: —

To-morrow, and to-morrow, and to-morrow,
Creeps in this petty pace from day to day
To the last syllable of recorded time,
And all our yesterdays have lighted fools
The way to dusty death. Out, out, brief candle!
Life's but a walking shadow, a poor player
That trusts and frets his hour upon the stage
And then is heard no more: it is a tale
Told by an idiot, full of sound and fury,
Signifying nothing.

Hemingway also gave us a profound narrative image of despairing nihilism in one of his most loved and anthologized short stories, "A Clean, Well-Lighted Place." The older waiter of the café says he cannot sleep because of insomnia, but he's really afraid of dying.

"What did he fear? It was not fear or dread. It was a nothing that he knew too well. It was all a nothing and a man was nothing too," wrote the omniscient narrator, as he peeks voyeuristically into the old waiter's soul, and Hemingway even has him mocking the Hail Mary prayer (and all religious notions of an immortal soul and life after death): "Hail nothing full of nothing, nothing is with thee…"

Professor Bloom was prescient in his *Anxiety of Influence*. Writers are influenced by former writers and try to expand and improve upon them, and Hemingway was influenced by the spirit of nothingness in Macbeth's famous soliloquy. Hemingway brought it close to home in the old waiter, who was afraid of dying because he did not want to be swallowed up by the nothingness of his life; but try as he may to stave off the spirit of nothingness with his voracious appetite for more life, Hemingway finally broke down and killed himself, not like the old man who drank himself drunk every night in the clean, well-lighted café who tried to kill himself by hanging, but by blowing his brains out with a shotgun...

13. Expanding the Paradigm

Monday, April 10, 2017

I can't get over my fascination with Professor Bloom, and I have gone to bed many nights with him on my mind, the tragic sound of his voice haunting me to sleep, and I'm looking forward to his next book whose working title he said was "Possessed by Memory" but which will probably be changed by his publishers, if he gets to finish it because he's in his late eighties and sounded very feeble in his last interview; but my fascination for him goes beyond his tragic inability to resolve the paradox of man's dual nature that Shakespeare expressed more sublimely than any other writer in Hamlet's "To be or not to be" soliloquy, it's also because of his gift for speed reading and preternatural memory.

Professor Bloom amazes me so much that I see him as a freak of nature, and I mean this in the best possible way, a literary savant who seems to have been born with the soul of literature that awakened in his precocious youth when he started reading poetry, because how else can a mere lad eight or nine read Hart Crane and Shakespeare and be moved by them?

It can take a lifetime to understand Hart Crane's poetry, if one can even crack it, and more than a lifetime to absorb the genius that is Shakespeare which Professor Bloom did his best to do, but for a pre-pubescent boy to read the great poets so early in life speaks to something that I have to address, because I cannot accept his explanation for his unbelievable reading skills (he could read up to 1000 pages in one hour in his thirties which slowed down to a mere 500 pages an hour in his eighties) and incredible memory (he can recite Milton's *Paradise Lost* and recall at will whatever poetry or prose that impacted him), gifts that he attributes to genes passed on to him by uncles who were Talmudic scholars; no, there's more to Professor Bloom than this, something that speaks to the mystery of our *becoming…*

I believe in reincarnation. This is not a concept that I embraced because it offered me a more satisfying explanation for why we are the way we are than any other belief system, including Buddhism whose concept of reincarnation denies the existence of our autonomous self which I happen to believe in (*indeed, it was because of my belief in the autonomous individual self that I went on my quest for my true self*); I embraced reincarnation because I was ready to bring my karmic cycle of lives to resolution, and which I've written about in all my books, my most recent being *Death, the Final Frontier* and *The Merciful Law of Divine Synchronicity.*

I had four past-life recollection dreams in high school, which awakened me to reincarnation (I didn't know these dreams were memories of my past lives until I discovered what Socrates called the "doctrine uttered in secret" when I left high school and read Edgar Cayce), and when Penny and I moved to Georgian Bay fourteen years ago I had seven past-life regressions, so reincarnation is not a concept for me; it's the secret way of life, period. This is why professor Bloom intrigues me. I'm convinced that he's a savant of literature because of his past lives just as Mozart was born with a genius for music, Einstein with a genius for mathematics, and other gifted souls who from lifetime to lifetime evolved in the *daimonic* genius of their own individual consciousness, so too was Professor Harold Bloom born with a genius for literature, which explains his preternatural attraction for poetry.

Professor Bloom is Emersonian in his belief about life, holding that "There is no next life. Here and now is the whole fact." But that does not negate the principle of reincarnation, which can only be realized in this world. In fact, it's because "here and now is the whole fact" that makes the Shakespearean "breathtaking kind of nihilism" so tragically poignant, because the exit out of the "here and now" cannot be found until one completes what nature cannot finish, which is to realize one's true self; and this is the irony of Professor Bloom's dilemma.

Professor Bloom made a telling comment about Hart Crane, whose poetry he reveres like sacred text, telling us that Crane read Ouspensky's book *In Search of the Miraculous* which Professor Bloom found "unreadable," but by some strange coincidence choreographed by the gods of literature, this just happened to be the same book that *the merciful law of divine synchronicity* brought into my life which introduced me to Gurdjieff's teaching of self-transformation that initiated me into mysteries of the secret way; so I'm led to wonder if the good Professor, who calls himself a Jewish Gnostic, shied away from literature that would have directed him to take evolution into his own hands to resolve the paradox of his life that kept him bound to the labyrinth of life and the breathtaking nihilism of literature, because it seems to me that Bloom's sacred poet Hart Crane was exploring the same path that Katherine Mansfield and I explored in Gurdjieff's teaching, but Crane's conflicted life derailed him.

I've got two books on Hart Crane on my Amazon wish list, *Hart Crane: Complete Poems and Selected Letters,* and *The Broken Tower: The Life of Hart Crane*, by Paul Mariani, which I will be ordering with some other books on my wish list, because I have to read this poet and his life story just to see what Professor Bloom saw in him when he was given a copy of Crane's complete poems when he was only twelve years old and has been reading, teaching, and writing about ever since. I suspect I know the answer, but I still need more context to proffer an explanation. I can offer a hint though, and it has to do with the "hidden path" that Crane intuited with his *daimonic* compulsion to write poetry which "led" him to the secret way of life that flowed through his inspired poems that could have saved him from himself had he not been so conflicted...

14. The Secret that is Literature

Tuesday, April 11, 2017

Had not my call to writing been supplanted by my call to find my real self, I would never have discovered the secret that is literature, because in my quest for my real self I was awakened to the secret way of life that is the archetypal imperative of literature. But this is such a complex story that it has taken me more than twenty books to bring it to light, which I hope is palpable enough to give my quest for my real self reader-credibility.

It's easy to dismiss a writer's truth, regardless how palpable they try to make it; that's why some writers resort to magical realism when their truth strains the limits of normal fiction and autofiction. Autofiction combines autobiography and fiction, much like my novels *Tea with Grace* and *Healing with Padre Pio;* but my novel *The Golden Seed* falls into the genre of magical realism, because I had to make the central experience of my story as palpable as possible to make it credible for the reader. Which wasn't easy to do given my incredible experience.

The central experience of *The Golden Seed* was an experience that I had when I hit another impenetrable wall in my quest for my real self. I asked myself the question: *"How can I know for sure that the choices I make in my life are the right choices?"*

Should I major in philosophy, psychology, religion, or English literature? Should I stay in this job or look for another? Should I date this woman or not? Should I get a divorce or wait until the children are older? Should we buy a new house now or wait? We all have choices to make in life, but how can we be sure that the choices we make are the right choices?

I had no idea whatsoever, and I pondered my quandary for weeks if not months when I hit a brick wall when Gurdjieff's teaching came to a grinding halt; and then one day I had an epiphany when the old saying *"let go and let God"* spoke to me.

How many times have people flipped a coin to make up their mind for them? Should we do this or that? Let's flip a coin and let chance decide. That's what I did when I didn't know what to do, I flipped a coin when I was in doubt and let chance decide for me; that's how I broke the divine secret of letting go and letting God, which was such a powerful experience that the only way to make it palpable was to tell my story in the genre of magical realism, which became the inspiration for my novel *The Golden Seed.*

For twenty years I tried to write this story, but no matter how hard I tried I just couldn't get into it, as though it resisted me because I wasn't ready to write it. And then one day—actually, it was shortly after I completed my fantasy novel *Jesus Wears Dockers* and I had so much energy left over from my dialectical play with my archetypal Jesus that I picked up my pen and wrote the first chapter of *The Golden Seed,* and I knew instantly that this was my entry into my incredible experience of *letting go and letting God.*

My six-month experience of flipping a coin to make up my mind for me when I was in doubt about what choice to make initiated me into the divine mystery of what Emerson called "God within," because by letting go and letting God decide for me I engaged my "superior insight" and the coin always confirmed the gut feeling I had about which choice I should make. Not once, not twice, not three times, but every single time I flipped my coin it confirmed what I felt in my gut I should do!

The odds of the coin confirming my gut feeling every time I flipped the coin to decide for me were astronomical, and I had to attribute this to a higher power—to the "God within" that I took to be my Higher Self, or what Jung called my "superior insight."

"Heads I do, tails I don't," I would say whenever I was in doubt about a difficult decision; but I also had a gut feeling every time I flipped my coin about which choice I should make. And then I'd flip the coin and go with it, whatever the consequences. One time, for example, I was uncertain about asking a young woman on a date. I liked her, and I could tell that she had eyes for me; but my gut said no, and my flip confirmed it. AND THIS HAPPENED EVERY SINGLE TIME I FLIPPED THE COIN: IT ALWAYS CONFIRMED MY GUT FEELING!

And once I realized this, I stopped *letting go and letting God* because I had enough confidence in my gut feelings now to stop letting my coin decide for me—which, if my memory serves me (I will check this later, but I really don't think I have to), Carl Jung had a similar experience. When he was in doubt and needed confirmation, he practiced the ancient Chinese system of divination; but this practice sharpened his intuitive skills enough to stop relying upon the I Ching, which was one more reason why Jung became my hero…

How many times have writers confessed that they have worked out their problems through writing? That their writing was cathartic and healing? What is this mystery? How can the process of writing heal one's soul? Or one's mind, if one does not believe in the soul? Why did Hemingway say that he worked out many things by writing about them? Was that why he had to write every day? He needed the magic elixir of writing to keep him healthy and sane? What was the lure of writing for him?

Hemingway could lose it very easily, especially when drinking. He was often moody and unpredictable, and writing engaged his "God within" and kept him sane. But in the end he could not control all the demons that he had created with all of his betrayals and self-betrayals in his *daimonic* quest to be the greatest writer of his generation, and his wife Mary had to have him committed to the Mayo Clinic in Rochester for treatment, the excuse being his high blood pressure and depression but it was more for his paranoiac behavior.

But the ECT (Electro Convulsive Treatment) that Hemingway received for his deep depression affected his memory and writing ability, and if he couldn't write there was no more reason left for him to live. "What these shock doctors don't know is about writers and such things as remorse and contrition and what they do to them," he said to his friend Aaron Hotchner in a moment of despairing lucidity. "They should make all psychiatrists take a course in creative writing so they'll know about writers."

So there's much more to writing a good story than meets the eye, and this "much more" constitutes the mystery of the creative process that Emerson called "God within" that heals writers of remorse and contrition and many other personal demons.

This is what I intuited to be the secret that is literature, the "hidden paths" that literary critics like Professor Bloom try to connect from one poem to another, and one story to another, individual paths born of the writer's *daimonic* need to reconcile himself with himself; this is the secret way of life that is the archetypal imperative of literature…

15. The Mystery Dissected

Thursday, April 13, 2017

"In truly good writing no matter how many times you read it you do not know how it is done. That is because there is a mystery in all great writing and that mystery does not dissect out. It continues and it is always valid. Each time you re-read you see and learn something new," wrote Hemingway in a letter to Harvey Breit (*Selected Letters*, 1952); but Hemingway was wrong. The mystery does dissect out, if one *knows* the secret.

"Nobody really knows or understands and nobody has ever said the secret. The secret is that it is poetry written into prose and it is the hardest of all things to do," said Hemingway; but again, he was wrong. It may well be the hardest of all things for a writer to write the secret that is poetry into prose, but I *know* the secret that is poetry, and I suspect I was called back to Hemingway so I can write the secret into the stories I've been called to write but can't, like my kundalini experience in Annecy, France that awakened the "serpent fire" which took me the better part of ten years to harness, and even now the "serpent fire" still torments me when it is stirred from its slumber for such is the seductive power of sexual desire…

Yesterday I listened to an *Open Source Radio* podcast, Christopher Lydon's conversation with Professor Bloom on the poet Hart Crane whom Bloom read at the age of nine or ten (his sister gave him a copy of the collected poems of Hart Crane when Bloom was twelve, the first book that he could call his own because all the books he was reading were from public libraries), and Christopher Lydon innocently confessed his feelings about Hart Crane, "I must say, for me a hard nut to crack," which confirmed my own feelings when I tried to read some of Crane's poetry this morning; and Professor Bloom replied: "He gives you an impacted density, you might say, and it's very difficult to unravel an impacted density. Crane is one of those rare poets who does not develop, he just unfolds; and the poetry that he was writing at sixteen is already the kind he will write when he kills himself at thirty-two."

So how could a mere boy of nine or ten be so taken by Hart Crane's poetry when such a well-read septuagenarian like Christopher Lydon found him a hard nut to crack? That's why I had to listen to his conversation on Hart Crane with Professor Bloom again, and when I heard the good professor recite from memory Crane's poem "The Broken Tower," which he considered to be Crane's greatest poem, I felt the impacted density of the poem which led me to say to Penny this morning, "Poets aren't made. They're born with the gift of poetry."

I read "The Broken Tower" again while Penny was still sleeping and I waited for the coffeemaker, as well as three or four more of his poems, and I couldn't make heads or tails out of them and probably wouldn't have bothered reading Crane had not Professor Bloom held him in such high esteem; and listening to him unpack "The Broken Tower" only confirmed my feelings about Professor Bloom's own genius for literature, which is why I honestly believe that he was born a literary prodigy.

"I don't doubt that his phenomenal speed reading skills and amazing memory were genetically passed onto him by his ancestors, but I believe it has more to do with his past lives," I said to Penny this morning. "The same with people like Mozart and Einstein. They were the product of their past lives, and the same with gifted poets like Hart Crane…"

How else could Crane's poetry have such an impacted density? How else could he write the kind of poems at the age of sixteen that Professor Bloom felt he would write at the age of thirty-two? What was this impacted density that defined his poetry if not the unconscious knowledge of his unresolved past lives, his *daimonic* self?

That's what I tried to explain to Penny. "There can't be any other explanation than reincarnation. The knowledge of one's gift is presupposed, that's the only way one can explain a genius like Mozart or Einstein. But they're not conscious of this knowledge. You could say it's in their genes, but it's instinctive however they got it…"

I've grown to believe that the principle of reincarnation and man's biology work together just as that entity called Seth who was channelled by Jane Roberts explained in her books *Seth Speaks: The Eternal Validity of the Soul*, and *A Seth Book*, both of which I bought at the Thunder Bay Bookshop Co-Op Inc. & Record Store 43 years ago, on *October 24,1974*. I know this because I found the sales slip in one of the books when I took them out last summer to read again because Robert Moss had made a reference to *Seth Speaks* on his blog. I was reading Moss at the time. I have five or six of his books, my favorite being his autobiographical story *The Boy Who Died and Came Back*. Robert Moss is a "dream shaman" who gives dream workshops throughout the world, and I found his books *Conscious Dreaming* and *The Secret History of Dreaming* very informative and helpful; but as exciting as Moss's personal path was, it did all it could for me and I moved on.

But when Penny went to work later I took out my Seth books and found a passage I had highlighted where Seth confirmed my belief that our genetic make-up and reincarnational memory work together: "There are states of consciousness, one within the other, and yet each connected, of course, so that genetic systems are really systems of consciousness. They are intertwined with reincarnational systems of consciousness. These are further entwined with the consciousness that you recognize. *The present is the point of power.* Given the genetic makeup that you now have, your conscious intents and purposes act as the triggers that activate whatever genetic or reincarnational aspects that you need. The state of dreaming provides the connecting links between these systems of consciousness" (*A Seth Book, Volume 2: Dreams, "Evolution," and Value Fulfillment*, p. 326, Italics mine).

Since I read these books 43 years ago, I had this information in my subconscious; so what I said to Penny about our genetic makeup and reincarnational memory wasn't original, I just tapped into my subconscious memory data base and told her what I "felt." And that's what I think the born genius in their respective field can do, but only with them it's an instinctive gift of presupposed knowledge that they realized over many lifetimes. But this is very difficult to explain, and the best way to illustrate what I mean by "instinctive gift of presupposed knowledge" would be by way of my future-life recollection dream.

A few years ago I had a dream of a future lifetime in which I was born a very precocious, gifted writer. In my dream, I loved and studied words because words gave me as wide a conceptual understanding of life as my vocabulary allowed me, and I read incessantly and studied dictionaries and wrote poetry and stories before I was five; but my precocious gift for writing was born of my past lives, especially my current lifetime.

In my current lifetime, I devoted years to reading and writing despite my primary goal of looking for my real self, which I was fortunate enough to find; and I believe that all of my reading and writing in my current lifetime will be realized as an instinctive gift for writing, in my future life which I experienced in my dream. That's how our reincarnational memory serves our inherent need to realize what we are meant to be, and when we have realized what we are meant to be (our true self), then we devote our life to our highest purpose, which is to serve God by serving life with our special gift that we have realized over many lifetimes. That's the conclusion that I came to in my book *Death, the Final Frontier.*

This is why I believe Professor Bloom was born a literary prodigy with incredible reading skills and preternatural memory, a gift that blessed him with an instinctive awareness of the *daimonic* imperative of literature that allows him to "see" the "individual path" of every poem and story, and by "individual path" I mean the personal individuation process of the author's essential self as they work it out in their writing; but, unfortunately for Professor Bloom, his personal belief system will not allow him to see that the natural process of individuation will not satisfy the longing in one's soul for wholeness and completeness, because nature will only evolve one so far and no further; to satisfy this longing in one's soul one has to take evolution into their own hands, which was why Katherine Mansfield said that literature was not enough and sought Gurdjieff out to help her satisfy the desperate longing in her soul for wholeness and completeness. A very courageous thing to do.

Stuck in the labyrinth of literature, which Shakespeare mirrored best in what Bloom calls "a breathtaking kind of nihilism," Professor Bloom has an instinctive awareness and cognitive knowledge of the natural individuation process, as books like *The Daimon Knows* and *Shakespeare: The Invention of the Human* tell us; but literature falls short of fusing the soul, self, and me myself into one's essential self, and Professor Bloom cannot help but suffer "literary melancholia," as all people do when literature can do no more for them, and not until one learns the secret of taking evolution into their own hands will they free themselves from themselves and satisfy the longing in their soul for wholeness and completeness.

This is why I was called back to Hemingway three years ago when I "chanced" upon the television movie *Hemingway and Gellhorn* that inspired my book *The Lion that Swallowed Hemingway*, and again this Christmas when I was given the gift of an *Indigo Hemingway Notebook* from Penny's sister that inspired my story "Hemingway's Forgotten Notebooks" and this private journal on my writing life.

In *The Lion that Swallowed Hemingway*, I did my level best to prove (for myself, at any rate) that Ernest "Papa" Hemingway got swallowed up by his own shadow which drove him to despair and suicide; but in my call back again to Hemingway I can't help but feel that it has to be to better understand myself through creative writing, and I can only do this by delving deeper into the *enantiodromiac* nature of Hemingway's ego/shadow personality and offer a way out of the despairing nihilism of literature in my own stories and novels...

16. Hemingway's "Black-Ass"

Saturday, April 15, 2017

"We Poets in our youth begin in gladness, /But thereof come in the end despondency and madness," said Wordsworth in his canonical poem "Resolution and Independency," reflecting that "breathtaking kind of nihilism more uncanny than anything Nietzsche apprehended," as Professor Bloom described Shakespeare's view on life; but Wordsworth was aware of the *enantiodromiac* nature of man and saw his dark mood as the flip side of his happy nature— "But, as it sometimes chanceth, from the might /Of joy in mind that can no further go, /As high as we have mounted in delight /In our dejection do we sink as low; /To me that morning did it happen so; /And fears and fancies thick upon me came; /Dim sadness—and blind thoughts, I knew not, nor could name…"

We've all sunk into despair, dark moods that suck the joy out of life, and it takes uncanny wisdom to dispel them. Hemingway, who was subject to these dark moods most of his life but fell into them more quickly and more often as he got older, called these depressive moods his "black-ass" affliction, and he didn't know how to dispel it but to drink more, which only made him darker and moodier and more difficult to be with.

His third wife Martha Gellhorn could no longer suffer Hemingway's "black-ass," and had to leave him for her own sanity; but where did these depressive moods come from, and why did Hemingway, who had everything going for him, sink into them?

This is the mystery of the *enantiodromiac* nature of man…

Hemingway's first romantic love wounded him deeply, scarring him for life. Twenty years after nurse Agnes von Kurowsky wrote her letter to Ernest, who had returned a war hero to his home in Oak Park, Illinois waiting for her to join him, telling *"bambino mio"* that she had fallen in love with an Italian officer and couldn't marry him and was very sorry and hoped he could forgive her, he wrote in

"The Snows of Kilimanjaro," his most autobiographical story: "…the first one, the one who left him…how he had never been able to kill it."

Agnes's rejection broke his heart and he never forgave her. He tried to work out his pain by writing it out in his story "A Very Short Story," but he never got over the hurt of what she referred to in his story as "only a boy and girl love" (Agnes was seven years older than 19 year old Ernest) and it was for the best and hoped he would have a great career, which he did, thanks to what some of his critics called his best novel, *A Farewell to Arms,* in which his heroine Catherine Barkley, who was modelled upon Agnes von Kurowsky, died giving birth to her lover Frederic's child, a fictional rendering of Hemingway's unrequited love for Agnes.

In *The Hemingway Women,* Bernice Kert wrote: "Ernest wrote bravely to his friends about cauterizing her memory with a course of booze and women, but the rejection continued to rankle, until it became an emotional injury of enduring consequence." And "…ultimately he came to use his fiction as a way of dealing with trauma."

Hemingway rendered his entire life into fiction, that's how he processed his pain and pleasure, love and hate, guilt and remorse, fear and courage and every other mutation of his *enantiodromiac* nature into the self he longed to be, but not enough to satisfy the longing in his soul for wholeness and completeness, and he died bitterly unresolved when he could no longer live life on his own selfish, uncompromising terms.

But that's how Ernest Hemingway always lived his life, demanding the world to bow to his selfish expectations, and when he never got his own way he repressed his bitter hurts and disappointments and nourished his shadow that pervaded his massive ego, making him moody, irascible, and unpredictable; that was the source of Hemingway's "black-ass" affliction which grew in proportional intensity with the shadow side of his personality.

The dark shadow side of the human personality is a mystery to the world, but it's not invisible, especially to writers who have an uncanny ability to see the shadow, as Dostoevsky did in his novel *The Double,* Robert Louis Stevenson in his novel *The Strange Case of Dr. Jekyll and Mr. Hyde,* and my favourite in this genre, *The Picture of*

Dorian Grey by the author whom Profess Bloom calls "the sublime Oscar Wilde."

The shadow is a Jungian term and key to understanding depression, despite medical science's contention that it is neurological and chemically based, and not until one comes to terms with the shadow side of their personality will one be free of surprising mood swings and debilitating bouts of depression; that's what I tried to reveal in *The Lion that Swallowed Hemingway,* and what my new call to Hemingway seems to be confirming as I delve deeper into his complex personality and his short stories and novels…

17. My Personal Heat

Monday, April 17, 2017

I picked up my weekend papers Saturday morning, Toronto's *Globe and Mail* and the *National Post* (*Saturday, April 15, 2017*), and when I got home I sat on the front deck (it was a bit cool, but I love reading in the fresh air) and turned to Conrad Black's column first in the *National Post* (the paper he founded and later sold) because I've been following his career for years and love how the most humiliating experience of his life (he was charged with fraud and obstruction of justice and served 37 months in an American prison) humbled his off-putting, over-inflated ego and initiated a *metanoic* change of heart that endears him to me now because he no longer speaks from his entitled position of power and status (he does have peerage and is formally addressed as Lord Black) but more from the heart, and he's forever taking up the cause of the underdog in his weekly column, and I love him for it; and after I read the *National Post* I turned to the *Globe and Mail* and read Mark Medley's interview with the Canadian writer Barbara Gowdy's return to the literary world with her new novel *Little Sister* after an absence of ten years and I couldn't help but feel sorry for her situation.

Barbara Gowdy suffers from incurable back pain and wrote her new novel laying on her back for maximum comfort. She's been to doctors and therapists and tried all kinds of cures, but nothing works, and she suffers and takes pain killers and anti-depressants. Not a pleasant way to live. So the life-questions that she asks, which she calls "the basic existential questions," seem much more relevant: "Why are you you, and I'm me? Why aren't I you? Who are you? And who am I? These have always concerned me and my work," she said, as they do every writer who takes their work seriously because the creative process by virtue of its inherent imperative of reconciling our dual nature compels us to ask them.

Gowdy said that she always had "a preoccupation with the body and the mind. Why this body? Why this mind? Why this body in this mind? I've never really come to terms with it," and she writes fiction to work out her existential questions—and for therapeutic reasons as well, writing to take her mind off her ever-present back pain.

"Writing saved me," said Gowdy, and then explained: "It's kind of a meditation. You're in the moment. You're in the word. You're in the sentence. I could kind of forget my pain when I was writing," which all creative writers do, especially writers like Hemingway whose uncompromising selfish nature generated tons of grief for himself and his wives and children, especially his gender-conflicted son Gregory, and all the friends that he alienated when they failed to meet his expectations. This is why he said to his friend Scott Fitzgerald to help him out of his creative slump, "...when you get the damned hurt use it—don't cheat with it. Be as faithful to it as a scientist." If anything, Hemingway was a religiously devoted writer, and material was material however he came by it.

"There always seems to be something going on with me and my body that I'm not quite happy about. You go, when you write fiction, where the heat is. And that's where my personal heat is," said Barbara Gowdy to Mark Medley, and my personal heat was the irrepressible consciousness of my inauthenticity which surfaced in high school and fueled my quest for my real self which I wrote about in *The Summoning of Noman,* my story of self-reconciliation that was inspired by my *daimonically* charged poem "Noman" that I wrote in grade twelve a week or so after I read the anonymous morality play *The Summoning of Everyman.*

I jumped out of bed one morning and sat at my desk and the poem "Noman" poured out of me like molten lava pouring out of the mouth of a volcano, and I wrote with a fury I could not control, and in words that sounded biblical; but I had no idea what my poem meant, all I knew was that I was Noman and I was summoned to God for a reckoning.

God asked me for his "fish's scale" (which took me years to see that this was a symbol for my lost soul), but I did not have it to return to God, and God gave me three days to find it in an abyss with four corners; but because it would take one full day to search each corner of the abyss, it meant that if I didn't find my lost soul within three days I would suffer God's wrath. And I searched, and searched, and searched, and at the end of the third day I had to answer to God when he asked me, "Hast thou my fish's scale?" that I had not, and God condemned me to the fourth corner of the abyss to find my lost soul. And that's the story of my current lifetime which was prophesized in my *daimonic* poem "Noman."

No wonder then that in that same year in high school when I read Maugham's novel *The Razor's Edge* I was moved to awe and wonder by Larry Darrell's spiritual quest and became inflicted with the immortal wound that ignited my quest for my lost soul, and that's where my personal heat for all of my writing has come from...

18. This Isn't Theory

Tuesday, April 18, 2017

In the conclusion of the preface to his book *The Search for Roots: C. G. Jung and the Tradition of Gnosis,* Alfred Ribi wrote: "What I experience I do not need to believe; experience is the self-evident fact. With my experience, I stay on firm ground..."

I dropped out of university where I had gone to study philosophy in my quest for my real self because by the second semester of my third year I felt myself cast adrift in a sea of endless philosophical speculation; brilliant but endless, and I feared drowning. Desperately alone and terrified of what to expect out there, I needed *terra firma* to stand on, and with Gurdjieff's teaching of "work on oneself" I dropped out of university and vowed to build my life upon the truth of my own experiences; thus began my quest in earnest for my real self.

In retrospect, I now believe that I was called to go to university where serendipity could work its magic and introduce me to the teaching that changed the course of my life, and when I began living my life within the paradigm of Gurdjieff's transformative teaching I began to experience life with what I can only call an esoteric perspective, because the more I "worked" on myself with *conscious effort* and *intentional suffering,* the more the shadow side of life revealed itself to me, to the point where I could actually "see" the shadow of another person's personality, a strange experience that opened me up to C. G. Jung's psychology.

The shadow is a psychic reality. It is no less real than the ego personality. But because the shadow is the unconscious side of the personality, it is not as visible. But over the years I made an observation about the shadow that rankles people, because this truth is the shadow's deepest secret: *the shadow is most real when it is least discernable.*

In other words, the better the shadow can conceal itself within its personality the more freedom it has *to be*, which is the shadow's only imperative; and the more freedom the shadow has in its personality, the more shadow-afflicted a person will be, like my father.

My father was a shadow-afflicted man who could not control his demons, and his cowardly closet drinking put our family through hell; but that's material for a whole novel, if ever I get to write it. (Actually, I have written a short story called "Enantiodromia" that was inspired by Hemingway's story "Fathers and Sons.") Hemingway on the other hand was a public figure, and from all the biographies that I read on his life he was so hopelessly shadow-afflicted that his demons drove him to ultimate despair and suicide.

While waiting on my coffee pot this morning, I was nudged to read Siri Hustvedt's essay "Suicide and the Drama of Self-Consciousness," from her book *A Woman Looking at Men Looking at Women*, and she concludes her well-researched essay with the following words: "There is no simple answer to suicide, no easy way to explain it or prevent it. I am convinced, however, that it always 'has something to do with the other.' *It occurs in a zone between people and it turns on the profound need every person has to be recognized* (the shadow's voracious *need to be*). It may involve tender or brutal feelings or both at once. It can be rational or mad. And it always involves the imagination, the self as other, the self as seen as an object of love or hatred, pride or shame. Without this doubling of the self, without reflective self-consciousness, there is no one to kill" (*A Woman Looking at Men Looking at Women,* by Siri Hustvedt, p. 433, Italics mine).

I'm not a psychiatrist, nor a psychologist; I'm simply a writer who went on a quest for his real self and happily succeeded, and I can only speak from my own experience which has convinced me that the shadow side of the human personality is the missing X-Factor in the mysterious ailment of depression and tragic phenomenon of suicide.

Medical science can look for the "depression gene" and "suicide gene" until the cows come home, but the gnostic ground that I stand upon has convinced me that depression and suicide are more about our psychology than our biology, and not until the X-Factor is included in the equation no solution will be found for depression and suicide; *and by X-Factor I mean the unconscious shadow side of our personality...*

Alfred Ribi continues: "But can one experience something beyond the reach of extraverted consciousness? Consider this possibility. Every myth takes its origin in human inspiration. Inspiration—from the Latin *inspirare*—means a message from the spirit, the breath of life. The spirit is more than human; it speaks from the macrocosmos, the greater world, and not the limited world of our personhood. It can formulate truths of which we are not conscious. It can give us answers to the unanswered. So doing, it extends our personality into the immeasurable, into the infinite beyond time and space. By lifting us out of the restricted dimensions of our physical existence, the experience of such inspiration has a redeeming quality. Meeting this spirit, this inspiration, life fulfils a destiny beyond the dimensions of our sensible world. The Gnostics, if we understand their striving, can show us the way to this goal" (*The Search for Roots,* Alfred Ribi, Preface, p. x).

Being a writer, I know all about inspiration, and I'm very familiar with what James Joyce came to call "epiphanies," those surprising little moments of insight that pierce the veil of life and let us glimpse behind the scenes, like "seeing" the shadow in action which I began to do with uncanny frequency the more I "worked" on myself with Gurdjieff's teaching, my *Royal Dictum* (my edict of self-denial), and Christ's sayings which I incorporated into my transformative ethic of personal growth and self-realization.

"He that loveth his life shall lose it; and he that hateth his life in this world shall keep it unto life eternal," said Jesus in one of his most paradoxical sayings, which I apprehended more each day as I lived my edict of self-denial that I vowed to live for the rest of my life from the day it came to me in a moment of glorious inspiration on my lonely walk on the breakwater that day when I asked God what price I had to pay for truth and the spirit of inspiration gave me my edict of self-denial, which I called my *Royal Dictum*, by bringing to mind the words of Ecclesiastes (*"All the rivers run into the sea, yet the sea is not full; unto the place from whence the rivers come, thither they return again..."*) and Sophocles' play *Oedipus Rex,* the king who exiled himself out of his own kingdom.

This was in my second year at university, but from the moment I began to deny myself the pleasures of my life the more I "died" to my ephemeral self and "found" my real self. That's the gnostic wisdom of my life that awakened me to the shadow side of life, and I "worked" on myself long and hard enough to give birth to my real self one day in my mother's kitchen while she was kneading bread dough on the kitchen table; but I've written about this already in *The Pearl of Great Price* and need not expound upon it further...

19. My Journey to Authenticity

Wednesday, April 19, 2017

My whole life has been a flight from my shadow to my real self, beginning in high school. I first began to sense the presence of my shadow in the latter part of grade nine or early part of grade ten, and it never went away. It popped up every now and then in moments of uneasiness and distress and finally worked its way into my personality, and so concealed was it that not until I heard a voice in my mind ask me the question *"why do you lie?"* one night in my bedroom a year or so after I dropped out of university and Gurdjieff's teaching had brought me to dead end did I become aware of how false I had become, and my quest for my real self took a completely new turn, because from that moment on I began to question my every thought, word, and deed and saw how false I was and exerted all of my efforts to authenticate my life; and that became my path to my real self, forever seeking to transform the false in me into the real me, which I called my journey to authenticity.

I wrote a monstrous tome when I was well into my journey, called *Thoughts In Motion: Diary of a Holistic Runner (August 1, 1988-January 8, 1989),* which I gave Penny to read in the early stages of our relationship, a brutally insensitive request because she had just begun working as a bookkeeper for a Shopper's Drug Mart in Thunder Bay and was in the middle of her first year-end audit, but her fear of threatening our relationship if she did not read it compelled her to make time and I can never forgive myself for imposing myself upon her that way; but she has forgiven me, and she smiles at the whole wretched experience today while I still cringe at the blindness of my unbelievable conceit.

But that was just another example of the insensitive male ego that was so manifestly present in the life of my high school hero and literary mentor whom I'm reading about again in the wonderful biography *Paris Without End: The True Story of Hemingway's First*

Wife, by Gioia Diliberto, the formative years of Hemingway's life and apprenticeship…

Ego. We all know what it is, but do we understand it? What is the purpose of ego? Why does it want so much attention? Why is it so easy to see in others and not in ourselves? I spent my whole life trying to make sense of ego, and had I not been so pathologically committed to finding my real self I would never have resolved the issue of ego; but because I did, I can safely say that without ego we would never realize our destined purpose.

"As each plant grows from a seed and becomes in the end an oak tree, so man must become what he is meant to be. He ought to get there, but most get stuck," said Carl Jung, and when I got stuck (and I mean, really stuck!), a voice in my mind asked a question that alerted me to my false nature (*why do you lie?*), and that led me to believe in the presence of an inner guiding principle that Ralph Waldo Emerson called "God within" and Socrates called his "oracle" and Carl Jung called his "superior insight" and I finally came to call *"the omniscient guiding principle of life,"* which I expounded upon in my twin soul books *Death, the Final Frontier* and *The Merciful Law of Divine Synchronicity.*

Ego is as necessary to our individuation as the air we breathe, the water we drink, and the food we eat for our physical survival, because ego is how we harness the vital energies of life to nourish our evolving self-consciousness, and the more ego we have the more life force we can harness to grow into the person we are meant to be.

But because the natural process of evolution can only take us so far in our destined purpose, ego will one day cease to be a blessing and become a curse; and this is the paradoxical reality of the *enantiodromiac* process of our becoming which Jesus addressed in what Professor Bloom called his "dark sayings," like: *"If thy right eye offend thee, pluck it out and cast it from thee; for it is profitable for thee that one of thy members should parish, and not that thy whole body should be cast into hell."*

Where does a person go when his ego can do no more for him to realize his destined purpose? As Jung came to see through his many patients (and he treated some of the most powerful and successful people in the world), one gets stuck; and it was his professional calling to help his patients get unstuck so they could continue on to their destined purpose of becoming what they were meant to be. But what if one does not have a Carl Jung to help them get unstuck? What does one do then? Where does one turn?

We all get stuck on our journey to wholeness and completeness. Katherine Mansfield got stuck when she realized that literature could do no more for her, and she sought Gurdjieff out to help her find her real self; but not everyone has the wits, temperament, or courage to seek out a person or new teaching that will help them get unstuck, and they suffer existential despair like the pain-afflicted fiction writer Barbara Gowdy.

I, too, suffered existential despair, so much so that I vowed to find my real self or die trying; but in my journey of self-discovery I came to see that we are not alone in our quest for wholeness and completeness, and I say this upon the strength of the many times that I was given help by *the omniscient guiding principle of life* to get unstuck—but not always in ways that I recognized. Sometimes it took years for me to see the help I got, just as it will take years for Lord Conrad Black to see that his devastating public humiliation was the best thing that ever have happened to his over-inflated, status-established ego; and it was this realization that gave birth to one of my favorite sayings, which Professor Bloom might, in his forgivable conceit, also call dark: *Life is a journey through vanity to humility...*

20. Toujours le Legend

Thursday, April 20, 2017

According to her biographer Linda Simon, Alice B. Toklas, Gertrude Stein's lesbian lover and life companion, offers an insightful look into Ernest Hemingway's character with her first impressions of the young American writer who had been invited with his wife Hadley by Gertrude Stein for dinner shortly after the Hemingways settled in Paris, having been introduced to Gertrude Stein in a letter by Sherwood Anderson, thought Ernest to be "an opportunist concerned with creating and nurturing his own legend. *'Le legend, toujours le legend,'*" repeated Alice, which Hemingway's *daimonic* drive to be the best writer of his generation proved presciently and tragically accurate.

Without his first wife Hadley, Hemingway would not have become the legend that he became, the woman who gave him all the love, comfort, and financial support that he craved and needed in his formative apprenticeship years; but his drive for writing and lust for life caused cracks in his marriage, and Hemingway betrayed Hadley for her "friend" Pauline Pfeiffer, a betrayal that damaged Hemingway's soul from which he never recovered.

"I wish I had died before I ever loved anyone but you," wrote Hemingway in his memoir *A Moveable Feast;* and "in a way he did die," wrote Gioia Diliberto in *Paris Without End: The True Story of Hemingway's First Wife.* "He felt guilty about leaving her all his life. His betrayal of her seemed to damage his sense of himself as essentially strong and decent, and it sparked his creative and physical decline. After he left Hadley, Ernest's drinking increased, and he began to suffer from a variety of ailments that plagued him all his life. What's more, the boasting and cruelty that had always occupied corners of his personality took over and finally came to dominate Papa the world knows."

"The shadow goes by many familiar names: the disowned self, the lower self, the dark twin or brother in bible and myth, the double, repressed self, alter ego, id," wrote the editors of *Meeting the Shadow: The Hidden Power of the Dark Side of Human Nature,* Connie Zweig and Jeremiah Abrams. "We all have a shadow," they continue. "Or does our shadow have us? Carl Jung turned this question into a riddle when he asked: 'How do you find a lion that has swallowed you?' Because the shadow is by definition unconscious, it is not always possible to know whether or not we are under the sway of some compelling part of our shadow's content," which Ernest "Papa" Hemingway wasn't aware of...

I got the title of my memoir *The Lion that Swallowed Hemingway* from Carl Jung's question "How do you find a lion that has swallowed you?" Hemingway's shadow was the lion that swallowed him whole, and he was powerless to his menagerie of soul-crippling demons; that's why he fell into despairing bouts of depression that wore him down enough to take his own life in a manner suitable to the legend he had become, "a fearless man of action—war hero, athlete, lover, big-game hunter," and the best writer of his generation who finally wrested the Nobel Prize for Literature out of the hands of the Nobel Committee. As James Joyce once said of Ernest Hemingway in Gioia Diliberto biography of his first wife Hadley Richardson: "'He writes as he is…a big, powerful peasant, as strong as a buffalo. A sportsman. And ready to live the life he writes about. He would never have lived it if his body had not allowed him to live it." And live it, he did; that's why the grizzled writer said to me in my dream in Annecy, France: *"I have pissed out more life than you have lived."*

I loved the writer and hated the man, as many people did; but when serendipity blessed me with the movie *Hemingway and Gellhorn*, I had an epiphany that dramatically shifted my perspective on the man and the writer: I saw him for what he was, a tortured soul trapped in the *enantiodromiac* never-world of his own *becoming.* Ernest "Papa" Hemingway was living proof of Gurdjieff's "dark" saying: *"Happy is the man who has a chair to sit on, unhappy is the man who has no chair to sit on; but woe to the man who stands between two chairs."* Hemingway stood between the chair of his *being* and *non-being*, between his inner and outer self, between his lower and higher self, between his *essence* and *personality,* and the torment of being neither one nor the other drove him to such despairing bouts of "black-ass" depression that his only refuge was to shoot himself.

I stood between two chairs also, and I suffered unimaginable anguish; but I was driven by my *daimon* to find my real self, and nothing was going to stop me but my mortal demise, because that's what I came into this world to do. That was my destined purpose, and with Gurdjieff's teaching of "work" on myself I found my real self, which I captured in a poem that came to me upon visiting Penny's mother in the hospital: —

I Am

I felt ashamed of life when I saw her frail body
fighting for its life in the Emergency Room,
emaciated, and heaving like a bellows for air;
I saw no dignity in the physical struggle
to stay alive, no grace, no love, no honor,
just a bodily organism in the throes of death.
I walked home alone from the hospital,
the lonely moon as big as the Eye of God
and the stars sparkling like lost souls in heaven,
and I thought of life and death and everything
in between, and in my heart I smiled for all
of my efforts, struggles, and humiliations to find
my true self, because as I spied death steal my lover's
mother's life I knew, I simply knew that I am,
and life is merely something that I do.

Gurdjieff's metaphor of the two chairs speaks to the *enantiodromiac* process of our becoming, and not until one resolves the issue of one's ego-shadow personality can one transcend oneself and be the person they are meant to be: this is what my book *Gurdjieff Was Wrong But His Teaching Works* was all about.

According to Gurdjieff, man is not born with an immortal soul; but he can create one if he knows how. That's what Gurdjieff's teaching offered. But whether man is born with an immortal soul or not, Gurdjieff's teaching of self-transformation works all the same;

and by "working" on oneself one can take evolution into their own hands and complete what nature cannot finish. I did, and I know that his teaching works; and it's from this perspective that I wrote *The Lion that Swallowed Hemingway*, because for all of his creative genius and lust for life my high school hero and literary mentor died tragically unresolved.

Only writing gave him some temporary measure of resolution as he worked out his demons through his stories and novels, but not enough to satisfy the longing in his soul for wholeness and completeness, and when he could no longer write he shot himself.

Grace under pressure? Maybe, maybe not; that was the path he chose to live, and who am I to say that he had not written this into the script of his legendary life?

21. The Dark Sayings of Jesus

Friday, April 21, 2017

Speaking with Christopher Lydon on *Open Source Radio* for his provocative book *Jesus and Yahweh: The Names Divine*, Professor Bloom describes Jesus as he perceives him in the Gospel of Mark: "Here is someone who is portrayed as always speaking in enigmas, riddles, parables, dark sayings of one kind or another." Why would he call the sayings of Jesus "dark"? Is it because he was unable to penetrate their meaning? Were they dark because he could not "see" or "hear" their hidden message? And why did Jesus have to hide his message, anyway? Why did he say, *"Many are called but few are chosen?"*

Professor Bloom said he read the Bible, both the Old and New Testament, as literature, like he read Shakespeare, and that Yahweh was a fictional figure created by the authors of the Bible like Shakespeare created King Lear, something that would never have occurred to me had not Professor Bloom brought it to my attention, and though the Gospel writers Matthew, Mark, Luke, and John had never met Jesus, he was not a fictional character despite what some people believe, like the recently deceased Tom Harpur who advanced the theory that Jesus was a mythical and not historical person in his controversial book *The Pagan Christ*.

I read *The Pagan Christ* when it came out because Tom Harpur's journey of self-discovery interested me, starting with his book *Life After Death* in which he professed to not believe in reincarnation: "...the more I read of alleged past lives the more convinced I am that these are the induced products of the imagination, repressed memories, and what Jung calls the collective unconscious of the participants in these hypnotic regression" (*Life After Death,* by Tom Harpur, p. 256); and yet, a few pages later he boldly writes: "I believe the evidence shows that God rose Jesus up from the dead...It was a total transformation into an entirely new mode of being, a sign and a seal of a New Age to come. I believe the New Testament witness that, as he was raised, so too shall we all—and all humanity."

So Jesus was a real historical person for Tom Harpur when he wrote *Life After Death*, which was published in 1992, and for him the resurrection of Jesus happened; but when he published *The Pagan Christ* twelve years later in 2004, he no longer believed that Jesus was a living person; for Tom Harpur Jesus had now become a mythical figure like the Egyptian hero "Horus or Osiris who was the embodiment of divine goodness, wisdom, truth and purity." And as for reincarnation, the former Anglican priest/journalist Tom Harpur's hard views had softened: "I have thought a lot about reincarnation since I argued the case against it in *Life After Death*, but I have been challenged to examine the theory much more closely through the latest research. I still have not made up my mind" (*The Pagan Christ*, p. 192).

But he did believe in an afterlife. "My belief in a glorious dimension of life yet to be revealed—a life beyond death—is even stronger now than it was when my book on the subject appeared over a decade ago...we are all 'sparks of divine fire struck off from the flint of the Eternal,' immortal souls clad in mortal bodies," he writes in *The Pagan Christ*; so it's obvious that Tom Harpur's belief system was evolving, as does every person's because this is how the natural evolution of the *enantiodromiac* process of our becoming works—until, that is, we are ready to take evolution into our own hands and complete what nature cannot finish. And this is where the "dark" sayings of Jesus come into the picture, which I hope to demystify out of my deep respect and love for Professor Bloom, but only after I share another memory, though somewhat embarrassing, of the unresolved author of *The Pagan Christ*.

I didn't expect today's journal-entry on my writing life to tap into my memory of Tom Harpur's personal journey of self-discovery, but I feel I have to reveal that I wrote a book called *Dear Jesus*, a long discursive open letter to Jesus Christ, which I foolishly sent to my brother to read because we had established a correspondence relationship; but unbeknownst to me, my brother sent it to Tom Harpur to appraise (which cost my brother four hundred and fifty dollars) just to see what his professional opinion about getting it published would be, which was not very encouraging and quite off-putting, and I believe I still have my brother's letter somewhere stating this, but this of course only added to my fascination for Tom Harpur's personal journey, and when I read *The Pagan Christ* I felt giddily vindicated.

Tom Harpur was a genuine spiritual seeker, and he was called to his journey of self-discovery through the Anglican ministry, and he became the Religion Editor for the *Toronto Star* for 12 years which led to his weekly opinion column on ethics and spirituality that ran for 30 years, and then he wrote a regular column for the *Sun Media* chain of 26 papers in Ontario, plus a string of books chronicling his personal journey; but all of his questing and scholarly research confused him, which when looked at through the prism of Christ's "dark" saying , I can't help but feel that Tom Harpur was called but not chosen *"because strait is the gate, and narrow is the way, which leadeth unto life, and few there be that find it..."*

22. My Own Muddled Confusion

Saturday, April 22, 2017

This is the kind of stuff that has to be written as fiction because it cuts so close to the bone it would scar the author for life, which is probably why I've been called back to Hemingway again so I can translate the most private and secret experiences of my life into fiction because, as Alice Munro said and every writer comes to see eventually, *"Memoir is the facts of life. Fiction is the truth of life,"* and to do justice to the most private experiences of my personal journey I could only give them light through the art of fiction like my high school hero and literary mentor did when, for example, he worked out his androgynous sexual desires in his posthumously published novel *The Garden of Eden.*

Nonetheless, I can't paint a devout and scholarly seeker like Tom Harpur "confused" without explaining what I mean by the "dark" sayings of Jesus, because had it not been for Gurdjieff's teaching of "work" on myself I might well have ended up like I did in my past lifetime in ancient Persia, a wandering fool spouting the Koran and Rumi and crazy verses of my own making until I died of madness and malnutrition; so Tom Harpur's mental confusion (which, incidentally, was not my observation but St. Padre Pio's when Tom Harpur's name came up in one of my sessions with the psychic medium who channeled the saint for my novel *Healing with Padre Pio*) was mild compared to my muddled confusion that I had to work my way through after I had awakened the "serpent fire" in Annecy, France.

The "serpent fire" combusted my mind into a roaring blaze of insatiable desires, and I "played" out fantasies in my mind and "automatic writing" that I have neither the heart nor courage to talk about; but anyone familiar with the subject of the kundalini will know what I mean, because once the chakra at the base of the spine has been opened all hell breaks loose. So Tom Harpur may have been mentally confused in his spiritual quest, but not until one experiences the psychic fire of the kundalini can one really know the mental confusion one can fall into; and had it not been for my trade of house painting and drywall taping (I also did carpet cleaning for extra money), all very physically grounding work, plus seven and a half years of long distance running along the shoreline of Lake Helen on the outskirts of my hometown of Nipigon, I would probably have ended up as I did in my tortured and confused past lifetime as a wandering mad Sufi in medieval Persia.

My name was Salam, and I was about to be initiated into a secret sect called the "Order of the White Tiger" (I have no empirical proof that such a sect existed, but my past-life regression was too real to be dismissed as collective memory or fantasy); but I failed to pass my third and final test for my initiation because I could not master my "two stallions of desire" (my desire for God and sexual pleasure), and torn apart by the conflict in my soul I fell into that kind of "mystical" madness well-known in those times and culture that branded me a "fool of God" and which granted me the freedom to roam the streets and beg for food, and I went out of my mind and eventually starved to death.

But that was the experience I needed to continue on my journey to wholeness and completeness, because had I not had that experience I would not have known what it was like to be so mentally confused; and I had this past-life experience in my unconscious to draw upon to help me overcome the mental confusion I fell into when I accidentally awakened the kundalini from its primal slumber which set my mind on fire…

Mental confusion happens to everybody, but not to the extreme that I experienced after the "coiled serpent" crawled up my spine and set my mind on fire. Actually, it did not crawl up my spine; it felt more like a bubble floating up the canal of my spine, which happened accidentally when I did a meditation on a maple leaf that I had picked up one afternoon when I picked up my friends young children Patricia and Sabrina from school.

This happened on *October 21, 1968* in Annecy, France. I know the exact date because I recorded my experience on the back and front covers of the novel I was reading, *Wuthering Heights* by Emily Bronte; but I have quoted my kundalini experience in one of my memoirs already and need not do so here. Suffice to say that I have the immediate memory of this experience on record as I wrote it down in my paperback copy of *Wuthering Heights,* which I shared with no-one until I wrote about it many years later after I had completed my journey of self-discovery and was no longer in danger of slipping into a delusory world of make-believe; but I did write a short story implying my torturous experience in which I tried to help a young man who got pulled into his own mind like I had experienced.

One day on my way to give an estimate for a house-painting job, I saw Mark standing on a street corner in the rain talking to himself, but his lips weren't moving; and on my way back from my estimate an hour later he was still standing in the rain muttering away, and I picked him up and shocked him with my awareness of his mental condition, which he thought he was concealing from the world; and I took him out for a long drive to Five Mile Park on Highway 11 along the shores of Lake Helen and implored him to get professional help; but three weeks later they found his body in a room he had rented in a local hotel. He was married and had three children, but too proud to get help he overdosed and killed himself.

Like Mark, the delusory fantasy world of my own mind was one of the deepest and darkest secrets of my life, which I managed to conceal from the world too; but it gave me so much to work with as I "worked" on myself with Gurdjieff's teaching that the Herculean efforts I had to make every single day to keep from getting trapped in the fantasy world of my own making kept me from going mad like I did in my past Sufi lifetime, and in the most ironic sense I can call that whole confused period of my life a blessing in disguise.

The efforts I had to make every day to keep from not being sucked into my fantasy world created a relentless tension between Yes and No, and with Gurdjieff's techniques of *self-remembering* and *non-identifying* I "harnessed" the psychic energies of all this tension (should I indulge in my fantasy world or not, and dear God was the desire compelling to play out my fantasies in my mind, like an addict needing a constant fix!) and used it to create what Gurdjieff called a "Work self" which facilitated what he believed would be the "creation" of my own soul but which in reality simply nourished my already existing soul self until I had grown enough in self-consciousness to burst free from the *enantiodromiac* confines of my *being* and *non-being* (what Gurdjieff called my *essence* and *personality)* and realize my individuating soul self, which I finally did one fine summer day while talking to my mother as she was kneading bread dough on the kitchen table.

It happened innocently enough, so innocently in fact that I hardly knew what had just happened other than that I simply got a quiet overpowering feeling that I was immortal and would never die. I *knew,* I simply *knew* that I was *me* and would never die. And from that moment on I no longer craved to satisfy the desperate longing in my soul for wholeness and completeness, and I swear to God I never again ever felt lonely, and this is what I put words to years later in my poem "I Am" that reflects my journey of self-discovery…

23. Both but Neither

Jean Paul Sartre could not resolve the *enantiodromiac paradox* of his dialectical "I am what I am not and I am not what I am," but I did by "working" on myself with my *Royal Dictum* (my edict of self-denial), Gurdjieff's self-transformative teaching, and the "dark" sayings of Jesus; and I gave birth to my transcendent self one memorable day in my mother's kitchen, which allowed me to complete Sartre's nihilistic no-exit philosophy by expressing the gnostic reality of my journey of self-discovery in the following words: *"I am what I am not, and I am not what I am; I am both, but neither: I am Soul."*

I had *become* my true self, fulfilling the promise of the "dark" saying of Jesus that his kingdom would come when the two are made one: "For when the master was asked by someone when his kingdom would come, he said, *'When the two will be one, and the outer like the inner, and the male with the female, neither male nor female.'* (*The Unknown Sayings of Jesus,* by Marvin Meyer, p. 95); and "making the two into one" is what taking evolution into one's own hands is all about. That's how one completes what nature cannot finish.

And herein lies the problem for my high school hero and literary mentor, because the great Ernest "Papa" Hemingway had created such a chasm between his inner and outer self with all of his betrayals and self-betrayals that he could never bridge it, not even with his great passion for writing, and he suffered unbearable anguish which drove him to drink as much as he did to assuage his guilty conscience; but unable to expiate his guilt, his demons pulled him into despair so deep that he could see no way out but to kill himself...

Do I have a right to proffer this perspective? What professional qualifications do I have to analyse the great writer who thought all "shock doctors" should take a course in creative writing "so they'd know about writers" and "things as remorse and contrition and what they do to them." Ironically C.G. Jung, one of the founding fathers of depth psychology along with Sigmund Freud, knew about these things which he spent his whole life exploring and working out in his psychology of individuation; but Jung cuts to the quick with his psychology, and few people read him for fear of having to deal with their shadow.

That's why I made C. G. Jung and Ernest Hemingway the main characters of my memoir *The Lion that Swallowed Hemingway*, because I wanted to show Hemingway in the light of Jung's psychology—because Hemingway failed to find his true self, and Jung did.

"By following the messages appearing in our dreams, Jung believed that the path leading to self-realization and personal wholeness could be discovered," wrote Robert L. Van de Castle in *Our Dreaming Mind.* "His belief was affirmed in a dream he experienced just before his death. In it he saw, 'high up in a high place,' a boulder lit by the full sun. Carved into the illuminated boulder were the words 'Take this as a sign of the wholeness you have achieved and the singleness you have become'" (*Our Dreaming Mind,* by Robert L. Van de Castle, p. 145). And I too had a dream which confirmed my own journey of self-discovery. In my dream I looked up my name Orest Stocco in the dictionary; and when I found it, there was only one word to define who and what I was: Soul.

That's why I have such resonance with Carl Gustav Jung, because we both found the secret way of life and passed through the eye of the needle; and this is the only qualification that I need to unravel the mystery of the man and the writer, Ernest "Papa" Hemingway, who called me to writing in high school and keeps calling me back again…

24. Hemingway's Tragic Flaw

Monday, April 24, 2017

I get the *Toronto Star* delivered to our house every weekend, but Sunday's home-delivery *Star* does not contain the two inserts *The New York Times International Weekly* and *The New York Times Book Review*, both which I look forward to reading, which is why I have to go out and buy another copy of the *Sunday Star* off the shelf because it contains these inserts; and something that I read in *The New York Times* insert jumped out at me because it spoke to the book I was reading on Hemingway's first wife Hadley Richardson whom he betrayed for the inveigling Pauline Pfeiffer who destroyed Hemingway's marriage.

In his article "Sheryl Crow Plays What's in the Mirror," the popular-music art critic for *The New York Times* Jon Paralese wrote: "Sometimes the comfort zone is where a musician belongs. That's the charm of 'Be Myself,' Sheryl Crow's new album, which unabashedly returns to the sound of her hit albums in the 1990s. 'This record, or all the records I've made, was just sheer joy,' Ms Crow said."

A lot of life happened to Sheryl Crow between her music in the 90s and her new 2017 album "Be Myself," and she attributes this to an experience that brought her face to face with her own mortality. "Treatment of breast cancer in 2006, she said, pushed her into savoring every moment. 'I don't know what I would have felt like if I had not had that moment of reckoning,' she said. '*My life shifted into something that was more authentic in a lot of ways*," concludes the article by Jon Paralese (Italics mine); and I purposively highlighted that passage because it spoke to Hemingway's tragic flaw that was fresh on my mind from my morning reading of *Paris Without End: The True Story of Hemingway's First Wife.*

My hatred for Hemingway's cruel and insensitive behavior in his betrayal of Hadley for Pauline was fresh on my mind when I read that article. I only had two more chapters left to read, but I had to put the book down because Hemingway's behavior, as guilt-ridden as it was, was also without shame; and Pauline's behavior—that was so wicked it fell into a category that one can only call evil, and many did call it just that.

I hated Ernest Hemingway for what he did to Hadley, but my hatred for Pauline Pfeiffer made me furious at myself for hating someone so much; but for me her sin was no less wicked than the heinous sin of pedophilia, both monstrous sins that robbed the innocent of their virtue, and there was an innocence to Ernest and Hadley's marriage that almost sanctified them. That`s what Pauline Pfeiffer had desecrated and alerted me to Hemingway's tragic flaw—his constant self-betrayals that robbed his soul of the precious virtue that he desperately needed to stay true to himself and authenticate his life, starting with the betrayal that damaged his soul for the rest of his life, his betrayal of Hadley's love for Pauline's.

But Hemingway always wanted to have it both ways, regardless of the damage he did to others; and people wonder where our demons come from. That's why I had to write a spiritual musing for my blog when I heard the novelist John Irving make the karmically obtuse comment, "You don't choose your demons, they choose you." I wrote "Chicken Little Syndrome and the World According to John Irving" for my blog, and then I included it in the fourth volume of my spiritual musings *The Armchair Guru* because I wanted to offer the perspective that we are the authors of our own misery.

That's what I took Hemingway's tragic flaw to be, his insatiable appetite for more life in his blind service to his *daimonic* need to become the greatest writer of his time, which when push comes to shove was why he abandoned Hadley for Pauline, because Pauline was younger, richer, embarrassingly more fashionable, and of invaluable service to the hungry young writer working on his novel *The Sun Also Rises* that launched his career.

And, of course, she also serviced his androgynous sexual needs by having Pauline cut her hair short like a boy, and whatever other wicked little games they played in bed just like he wrote about in his novel *The Garden of Eden*...

25. Paying the Piper

Tuesday, April 25, 2917

I love coincidences. Coincidences speak to the harmony of life, and when I experience a coincidence I know I'm in sync with my own destined purpose which is to heed my call to creative writing that my return to Hemingway has initiated, and the surprising coincidence that I experienced yesterday with my neighbor while I was reading on my front deck confirmed my call back to Hemingway and creative writing.

It was a beautiful day. The sun was shining, finally; and though the air was a cool it was still warm enough to sit on my deck to read, which I love doing. I was deeply engrossed in Michael Reynolds final volume on Hemingway's life, *Hemingway: The Final Years* which I had read once already, when my neighbor from down the street walking his two little terriers came into the driveway. "Nice one today," he said, as his dogs circled around his legs.

"Oh, hi Lenny," I said, not noticing him. "Sorry, I'm deep into Hemingway's life," I added, showing him the book I was reading. "And after I finish this one, I'm going to read about the women in Hemingway's life," and I showed him Bernice Kert's book *The Hemingway Women*, which I had already read for my book *The Lion that Swallowed Hemingway* but wanted to read again to refresh my memory.

Besides, books always seem to read differently the second time around, especially books on Hemingway and his own writing, and I was getting so much more from my re-reading of Hemingway that I began to suspect that this journal on my writing life was morphing into a sequel to my memoir *The Lion that Swallowed Hemingway*, as though I still had something to say about the *enantiodromiac* process of Hemingway's conflicted nature, which perhaps I do because since I wrote my book on Hemingway's monstrous shadow I had grown considerably in my understanding of the *enantiodromiac* process of our becoming.

I should explain what I mean by this concept before I mention the telling coincidence that I experienced with my neighbor yesterday when he got a call on his cell phone precisely when I was telling him about paying the piper, and by the *enantiodromiac* process of our becoming I mean the natural evolution of our identity that is realized through the constant daily friction of our inner and outer self—our *essence* and *personality* as Gurdjieff would say, or our *being* and *non-being*, like Hemingway's daily conflict with his shadow; which was why I was re-reading books on Hemingway's wives, because through his relationship with Hadley, Pauline, Martha, and Mary I would see how the dark side of his personality took over his massive ego and made life painfully contentious and difficult for them.

That's what fascinated me about Hemingway, his shadow self which no one but a student of Jungian psychology would appreciate. But not until the shadow is acknowledged as a separate and autonomous aspect of man's personality will a person like Ernest "Papa" Hemingway, whose dark side was so obvious to his four wives, increasingly more so with each marriage (Mary suffered his cruel shadow the most, but she was determined to be the last Hemingway wife and stuck it out to the bitter end), be understood, and all because of the selfish choices he made to sacrifice everyone on the sacred alter of his precious art.

The last time we talked, my neighbor Lenny told me about his son's marriage breakup, and I asked him how he was doing. Lenny, who was himself on his second marriage (his two sons were with his first wife and they had no contact with their mother, which made Lenny both father and mother to his children growing up), shrugged his shoulders—

"That's life," he said, and proceeded to tell me about how his current wife in her human-resources position would tell him about all the workers in the factory where she worked (which had over five hundred employees) who changed partners like changing socks.

"That reminds me of something I said to Penny this morning," I said to Lenny. "We were talking about accountability, how karmically obtuse people seem to be today, and by that I meant that people don't want to see the consequences of their actions when they make self-serving decisions, like cheating on one's partner because they can't control their libido. I said to Penny this morning, 'If you don't pay the piper, it will cost you down the road.'"

Just then Lenny's cell phone rang. *"There's the piper now,"* he said, with a big smirk on his face. It was his wife on her way home from work, who when I asked her a week ago if she would miss her job when she retired at the end of the month she replied, "I don't think so. I'll have him to boss around, won't I?" and she laughed a forced laugh.

Lenny smiled, but in his smile I saw more than what he wanted to reveal, and I replied: "Not too much, I hope. You don't want him to become a dishrag."

She gave me a funny look, and he snickered.

Lenny was right. It was his wife on the phone, which was why he said *"There's the piper now;* and I instantly replied, *"Wow! How's that for a timely coincidence?"*

Lenny's wife was going to be in Orillia in a few minutes and wanted to know if they needed anything from Walmart, but they didn't, and they talked for a minute or so longer, and then I explained what I meant about life exacting its dues when we refuse to pay the piper, like Ernest "Papa" Hemingway who fell victim to "black-ass" and suicide; but I don't think my neighbor Lenny appreciated the irony of the timely coincidence...

26. Hemingway's Literary Discovery

Thursday, April 27, 2017

Every writer knows that the creative unconscious has a mind of its own, but very few writers will admit it, let alone talk about it; like Hemingway when he was asked about his creative process: "If I have to talk about a book I have written, it destroys the pleasure I have from writing it. If the writing is any good everything there is to say has been conveyed to the reader" (*Hemingway: The Final Years*, by Michael Reynolds, p. 250).

He may be right, but that does nothing to enlighten us about writing. Fortunately, Hemingway does give us an insight into his creative process in *A Moveable Feast* when he talks about his apprenticeship to the craft of writing which he boiled down to the *one true sentence principle* that evolved into his personal code to *tell it the way it was*.

In a lonely room on the top floor of the hotel where he practiced his craft, the young Ernest Hemingway thought to himself as he looked out over the roofs of Paris: "Do not worry. You have always written before and you will write now. All you have to do is write one true sentence. Write the truest sentence that you know," and then the well-seasoned Nobel laureate writing the memoir of his apprenticeship days elaborates on his now-iconic *one true sentence principle*: "If I started to write elaborately, or like someone introducing or presenting something, I found that I could cut that scrollwork or ornament out and throw it away and start with the first true declarative sentence I had written. Up in that room I decided that I would write one story about each thing that I knew about. I was trying to do this all the time. I was writing, and it was good and severe discipline" (*A Moveable Feast*, pp. 12-13).

"No other writer of our time has so fiercely asserted, so pugnaciously defended, or so consistently exemplified the writer's obligation to speak truly," wrote Carlos Baker in *Hemingway: The Writer as Artist*. But creative writing is not journalism, and a story told in the manner of reportage as Hemingway did in *Green Hills of Africa* will not transport the reader to that place that Karen Blixen called "the truth above the facts of life."

Hemingway learned an invaluable literary lesson with his reportage novel *Green Hills of Africa.* It taught him that without imagination he did not have art, which was why when he was asked about imagination at the height of his career he replied: "It is the one thing beside honesty that a good writer must have. The more he learns from experience the more truly he can imagine. If he gets so he can imagine truly enough people will think that the things he relates all truly happened and that he is just reporting" (*By-Line: Earnest Hemingway*, p. 215).

This is reportage of a different kind. It is not a factual account of what happened, it is a factual account imbued with the magic elixir of imagination which has the mystical power to transform the facts of life into a deeper perception that raises the facts to the level of truth called art; and that was Hemingway's literary discovery which he proved following his African reportage novel with two of his most canonical stories: "The Snows of Kilimanjaro," and "The Short Happy Life of Francis Macomber" that were drawn from the same safari experience that gave birth to *Green Hills of Africa.*

Alice Munro, who also mastered the craft of writing, built her stories—or, perhaps to be more accurate, *entered* her stories from what the novelist Miriam Toews called a *"founding moment"* in her introduction to Alice Munro's book of short stories *Too Much Happiness* which Miriam Toews illustrates with one of her favorite paragraphs from the book: "Something happened here. In your life there are a few places, or maybe only the one place, where something happened, and then there are all the other places."

This place where something happened is the *founding moment* of all good stories; but what do stories mean? For Alice Munro "fiction is the truth of life," and Miriam Toews tells what stories mean to the Nobel laureate: "Munro's stories allow us to look at our little lives with a type of awe. It's a sleight of hand thing, **the Alice Munro effect**, in which she presents the sad and awful facts of life to us, implicates us in them, and then leaves us with the option of forgiveness or self-reproach, which is like leaving us at a fork in the road—alone and wondering—and in that way her stories never end" (**Bold italics mine**).

Coincidentally, three years ago on *Saturday, June 14, 2014* I posted a spiritual musing on my blog called "The Munro Effect," which I wrote long before I read Miriam Toews introduction to Munro's book *Too Much Happiness* (I find it curious that both Miriam Toews and I came up with the same term for the effect Munro's stories have on the reader), but rather than say what my personal concept of the Munro effect is, let me quote my spiritual musing which, coincidentally enough, also relates to Ernest "Papa" Hemingway: —

The Munro Effect

In *October 2013* Alice Munro was awarded the Nobel Prize for Literature "for her mastery of the contemporary short story," which renewed my fascination for this hitherto underappreciated genre, and I made a resolution to read one Alice Munro story every week until I read them all; that's how I discovered "the Munro effect."

Shortly after she received the Nobel Prize, I heard Shelagh Rogers interview Alice Munro on her CBC radio show *The Next Chapter*; and in the course of the interview Munro said something—I swear to God, it was as though the thought just dropped into her mind from a higher plane like a freshly minted gem of golden wisdom—that jolted me upright: *"Memoir is the facts of life. Fiction is the truth of life."*

I instantly jotted down the aphoristic wisdom of the creative genius that elevated Munro's work from mere craft to art, but I didn't know this until I began reading her stories—this time with a watchful eye for what made her a grand master of the short story that garnered her the most coveted prize in literature after winning the second most coveted prize in 2009, the Man Booker International Prize, three Canadian Governor General's awards for fiction, two Scotiabank Giller Prizes, and several others for her remarkable gift of storytelling; and it was one story in particular, the title story of her book *The Love of a Good Woman*, that awakened me to her secret that I came to call "the Munro effect."

My renewed fascination for the short story re-ignited my life-long interest in another grand master of the short story, the writer who became my literary mentor from the day I discovered him in high school so many years ago, Ernest Hemingway; and once again I delved into his writing, which I do at least once a year but this time with a renewed fascination that compelled me to dig deeper into his life to better understand the man to see if I could ferret out the secret of his genius like I had unexpectedly ferreted out Alice Munro's.

I began my hunt for Hemingway's secret with the last book that he wrote before taking his own life, the memoir that bared his soul and read like a last confession before his self-appointed meeting with his Maker, *A Moveable Feast*; and Hemingway's last words on the world-famous writer and insensitive bastard that he had become compelled me to dig deeper until I confirmed the secret of his genius in what I came to call "the Hemingway factor" and which I realized was absolutely necessary to enhance "the Munro effect," and by "Hemingway factor" I mean what he implied in his stories, not what he revealed; or what he referred to as the iceberg theory of writing that he discovered studying Cezanne's art when he lived in Paris as a young man.

So, just what do I mean by "the Munro effect" that I have now come to see characterizes all good stories? Meaning, the greater "the Munro effect" has upon a reader, the better the story will be; and by "Munro effect" I mean *an act of the imagination that transforms reality into a deeper perception of what is*, which Hemingway confirmed when he said that a writer must make a story "so real beyond any reality that it will become a part of the reader's experience and a part of his memory" (*Ernest Hemingway on Writing*, edited by Larry W. Phillips, p. 5).

Alice Munro's genius, like Ernest Hemingway's and all great storytellers, lies in her ability to transform the naked facts of life into stories that transcend life and become art, just as another master storyteller Karen Blixen confirmed when she said: *"Art is the truth above the facts of life."* But just what is this truth above the facts of life that writers ferret out with their stories? And how did "the Munro effect" put me wise to it? That's today's spiritual musing...

There's a mystery at the heart of the human experience, and every writer seeks to make sense of this mystery. They are magnetically drawn into the web of this mystery, and story by story they seek to unravel it; but there seems to be no end to this mystery, and writers continue to write stories year after year, decade after decade, and century after century. Some writers get so close to the mystery that they become mystical in their art of story-telling, like Paulo Coelho's story *The Alchemist.*

From a very early age I wanted to be a writer, but my calling was to become a seeker first; so my best energies went into seeking an answer to the mystery of life. After years of seeking, I found the answer that I was looking for; and that's when I wrote my first novel *What Would I Say Today If I Were to Die Tomorrow?*

The shocking effect that my novel had upon the people of my hometown taught me that people fear to see the dark side of their personality, which the eminent Swiss Psychologist C. G. Jung called the *shadow*, although they relish reading about the *shadow* of other people. This was brought home to me again recently by a comment voiced by a friend of mine who recognized herself in one of my books and did not like what she saw, "I don't feel safe anymore," she told another friend.

When Alice Munro was asked by Shelagh Rogers in an interview a few years before her Nobel Prize what the people of her hometown thought of her stories, she replied, "I don't know. They don't speak to me." And there's a story that the descendants of the people that the legendary humorist Stephen Leacock satirized in books like *Sunset Sketches of a Little Town* still harbor an abiding resentment for him; but this is true of most writers, especially Ernest Hemingway.

Hadley Richardson Mowrer, Hemingway's first wife, said of his first novel that launched Hemingway's career into literary stardom, "I lived through *The Sun Also Rises* and can remember almost the whole thing. The dialogue and situations are very true to what I recall happened" (*The True Gen*, Denis Brian, p. 55). Of course, the models for the people in *The Sun Also Rises* recognized themselves and resented Hemingway for using them in his story; but *The Sun Also Rises* was not memoir. It was an act of the imagination that transformed the lives of "the lost generation" and their wild and festive time in the Spanish town of Pamplona into a greater perception of their experience, thereby revealing the deeper truth of their private, secret lives; that's why they were so angry at Hemingway for using them in his novel.

Harold Loeb, who was the model for Robert Cohn in *The Sun Also Rises*, visited Hadley almost half a century after the novel's publication and told her that he was still hurting from Hemingway's portrait of him, and Loeb tried to set the record straight in his memoir *The Way It Was*; but as the literary historian Malcolm Cowley wrote to the author of *The True Gen* Denis Brian, "In *The Sun Also Rises* Ernest wasn't even trying to be fair. But he could be satanically accurate." Harold Loeb was so bitter for feeling wrongly portrayed that he could never forgive Hemingway; but we aren't all what we think we are or pretend to be, and that's what writers reveal in their fiction, as I did in my first novel *What Would I Say Today If I Were to Die Tomorrow?*

Hemingway held the magnifying glass of his imagination upon his experience with his friends in Pamplona where they had gone to see the running of the bulls, and they didn't like what they saw; that's why they felt betrayed. But Hemingway held his magnifying glass to himself as well and revealed the dark side of his own personality, like in his short story *The Sea Change* which he expanded upon in his posthumous novel *The*

Garden of Eden. Few people made the connection between these two stories, but they both implied the secret dark side of Hemingway's androgynous sex life. To a writer, no one is safe; including himself.

This is why people who recognize themselves in a writer's fiction feel betrayed; they don't want their secret life to be revealed. But this is how writers get to the truth of life, which can be devastating for people who think they have secret lives until they are pulled into a writer's imagination where all bets are off, as novelist Joyce Carol Oates revealed with her uncanny portrayal of America's beloved poet Robert Frost in her *November 2013 Harper's* magazine short story, "Lonely, Dark, Deep" which drew outrage from Frost family members and tightknit world of Frost scholars because Joyce's story showed the sinister dark side of Robert Frost's personality.

Over the many years of her lonely self-doubting apprenticeship, Alice Munro cultivated a talent for holding the magnifying glass of her imagination to life with such devastating artistry that we get to see a full *enantiodromiac* snapshot of the people she wrote about, and we always come away from her stories feeling a little wiser, a little safer; this is what I mean by "the Munro effect."

———

My spiritual musing "The Munro Effect" is now included in *The Armchair Guru,* my fourth volume of spiritual musings; but to bring this journal entry to resolution let me return to Alice Munro's title story "Too Much Happiness," which does its utmost to bring to light the mysterious factor that transforms and elevates the facts of life into the truth of art.

Sophia Kovalesky, a real-life Russian mathematician and novelist living in Russia around the end of the 1800s, is the protagonist of "Too Much Happiness," and she's talking about a new idea for a story. "There was a movement back and forth, she said, there was a pulse in life. Her hope was that in this piece of writing she would discover what went on. Something underlying. Invented, but not."

This "pulse in life" is the closest that Sophia Kovalesky, real-life mathematician and novelist, and Alice Munro and Ernest Hemingway and every creative writer, have come to defining the mystical factor of their stories that transforms and elevates the facts of life into the truth that is art, the secret way into the *enantiodromiac* process of our individuation, which is why Miriam Toews wrote in her introduction about the effect that Alice Munro has upon her readers: "Stories are there, hiding, dark, and troubled, but waiting for when we need them to rescue us," which is why writers write stories and readers read them.

But, sad to say, as salvific as stories may be, they cannot complete what nature cannot finish. Like Katherine Mansfield said to her editor/mentor A. R. Orage, "Literature is not enough." This is why I've been called back to Hemingway...

27. The Creative Impulse

Friday, April 28, 2017

What Alice Munro referred to as "the pulse in life" in her short story "Too Much Happiness"—which is "Something underlying. Invented, but not"—and which she also refers to as that "lump of complicated painful truth pushing at my heart" in a draft version of her story "The Moons of Jupiter" (I got this from Robert Thacker's biography *Alice Munro: Writing Her Lives*, p. 141), I refer to as *the creative impulse* which, as I've come to believe, has a mind of its own that is infinitely wiser than our workaday cognitive mind; which is why I learned—*nay, I trained myself!* —to engage *the creative impulse* in my writing.

The creative impulse is the mystery of life. Ralph Waldo Emerson called it "God within" and "Over-Soul," and C. G. Jung called it "superior insight." It has also been called our Higher Self, Inner Master, Inner Guide, and Oracle by Socrates; but by whatever name this intelligent guiding principle of life is called it is "a movement back and forth, a pulse in life," as the Russian mathematician/novelist Sophia Kovalesky described it in Munro's short story "Too Much Happiness," a "lump of complicated painful truth" pushing at the writer's heart; and it is this "lump of complicated painful truth" pushing at my own heart that I made a discipline of exploring in my personal platypus genre that I call spiritual musings.

I call my spiritual musings a platypus genre because they are a form of essay and journal writing that involves the paradoxical discipline of letting go and controlling (letting my creative unconscious flow freely but at the same time controlling what flows out of me); but I don't set out to write a spiritual musing like I would set out to write a short story or a novel, which take considerable cognitive thought; I have to wait for the idea of my next musing to "possess" me before I can give it creative expression, like the idea of "the Munro effect" that took hold of me after I read her story "The Love of a Good Woman."

Once the idea of "the Munro effect" took hold of me, I had to explore it in a spiritual musing, because that's what a spiritual musing is for me—a form of creative reflection that enlightens me on a subject that has grabbed my attention. I knew there was more to the concept of "the Munro effect" than I understood cognitively, so I set out to explore it by engaging the enlightening powers of my creative unconscious, just as a poet does when he gets an idea for a poem and then unpacks it in the writing of the poem.

I can speak from the experience of writing short stories, novels, poetry and spiritual musings, so I know the distinction of the creative process for each genre; and though they are all imbued by the enlightening power of the imagination, each genre is given expression according to the demands of that lump of painful truth pushing at the writer's heart.

A novel, for example, makes much greater demands upon a writer than a short story or a poem, and it requires great commitment to write a novel because the idea, which is the soul of the novel, must have all the latitude the writer can give it to bring the novel to fruition; which I know to be true because this is what I experienced writing my novels *Jesus Wears Dockers* and *St. Paul's Conceit*—both of which gave birth to their own titles only when the soul of each novel had been realized enough in their unfolding to give birth to their own identity which they announced to me in their new title. This is what led me to see that **a novel is a sophisticated form of higher thinking that gives birth to its own truth through the process of creative integration.** As Munro would say, that lump of complicated painful truth pushing at the writer's heart is given expression in the writing of the story, or novel.

The same can be said of all creative writing, like my spiritual musings, which I made a habit of writing every time an idea for a spiritual musing possessed me just so I could master the discipline of engaging my creative unconscious, which I also did with poetry; whenever an idea for a poem came to me, I jotted it down and then set out to unfold it. And from this I learned that every genre requires its own set of creative muscles, and the creative muscles that I exercised writing my spiritual musings always exhausted me because unpacking the idea was very demanding. That's why after I wrote my last volume *The Armchair Guru* I had to take a break for five or six months before writing any more spiritual musings.

I wrote close to two hundred spiritual musings that I published in three volumes (*Just Going with the Flow, Old Whore Life: Exploring the Shadow Side of Karma, Stupidity Is Not a Gift of God*) and the soon-to-be published fourth volume, *The Armchair Guru*, and I've become quite adept at engaging my creative unconscious; this is why I can speak with some measure of certainty on the mystical process of creative writing, and when all is said and done I *have* to believe that we all have "superior insight" (Jung also called it our "transcendent function") which when engaged, as writers and artists tend to do by virtue of their discipline, can bring to light a deeper truth than what our workaday cognitive mind is aware of.

This is why writers say that they write to get to the truth of life. This is what Alice Munro meant by that lump of complicated painful truth pushing at her heart, and what Hemingway meant when he said, "All good books are alike in that they are truer than if they had really happened and after you are finished reading one you will feel that all that happened to you and afterwards it all belongs to you..." (*By-Line: Ernest Hemingway*, p. 184); and this is why I'm convinced that the creative impulse has a mind of its own...

28. Chemistry of the Soul
(A Spiritual Musing)

Saturday, April 29, 2017

Not yet summer but nearing the end of what the poet T. S. Eliot called the cruelest month of the year, a dull grey dismal day too cold to sit on the deck to have a tipple or finish reading my book *Paris Without End, The True Story of Hemingway's First Wife*, so I asked Penny if she wanted to watch a movie on Netflix in the cozy comfort of my writing room. She said yes, and I found a movie called *The Light Between Oceans,* starring Michael Fassbender as the lighthouse keeper, whose portrayal of C. G. Jung in *A Dangerous Method* completely won me over, Alicia Vikander as the lighthouse keeper's wife, whom I didn't know, and Rachel Weisz who played the birth mother of the infant child in this poignant drama, and whom I fell in love with the first time I saw her starring with Ralph Fiennes in *The Constant Gardner,* and we cozied up in our two sofa reading chairs and watched the movie that so moved me to tears it stirred up the root of an idea that I've had gestating in my unconscious for several years, and that's the subject of today's spiritual musing....

I had unfinished business with Hemingway since I wrote *The Lion that Swallowed Hemingway,* or I would not have been called back to Hemingway by my relentless Muse to write this journal/sequel; and all my new reading on the iconic writer whose simple prose introduced the modern world to a new style of writing was giving me a deeper insight into the *enantiodromiac* process of Hemingway's conflicted ego/shadow personality, which was brought to light with spontaneous delight when Michael Fassbender, who played the lighthouse keeper Tom Sherbourne in *The Light Between Oceans,* had to wrestle with a moral dilemma that he knew in the pit of his stomach would one day come back to haunt him if he did not choose wisely, just as Hemingway did when he was torn between his love for his wife Hadley and the other woman he had unexpectedly fallen in love with, the glamorous Pauline Pfeiffer who ended up becoming his second wife.

"That's it!" I exclaimed, when the lighthouse keeper Tom Sherbourne chose against his gut feeling to comfort his grieving wife who had just suffered her second miscarriage, jarring Penny from her comfort. *"That's the human condition in action! That's the grinding of the soul that makes for great literature! That's the chemistry of the soul!"*

Penny was puzzled by my outburst, but I was excited, as I always am when an idea for a spiritual musing springs free from my unconscious, and I shot out of my chair and jotted down the title of my new spiritual musing in my *Indigo Hemingway Notebook* that Penny's sister had given me for Christmas— "Chemistry of the Soul."

But what was the lighthouse keeper's moral dilemma that set this idea free, a moral dilemma that by miraculous happenstance was no less soul-wrenching and life-changing than Ernest Hemingway's marital dilemma that I was just reading about again in *Paris Without End, The True Story of Hemingway's First Wife?*

First, let me spell out what I mean by this exciting, gnosis-laden idea "chemistry of the soul," and then I will explain how it was set free by the lighthouse keeper's moral dilemma that instantly brought to mind Hemingway's marital dilemma that I was all-too familiar with and coincidentally just happened to be reading about again in Gioia Diliberto's biography *Paris Without End, The True Story of Hemingway's First Wife.*

The phrase "chemistry of the soul" just came to me out of the clear blue when I made the connection between the lighthouse keeper's moral dilemma and Ernest Hemingway's marital dilemma, but this is the phrase that my creative unconscious gave me to capture my spontaneous insight of what a moral dilemma can do to one's soul, because I *knew* from all the reading I had done on Ernest Hemingway what his marital dilemma had done to him when he chose to betray his wife Hadley for his lover Pauline, which gave me the insight to foresee what the lighthouse keeper's moral dilemma would do to him if he made a decision that went against his gut feeling; that's why I burst out: *"That's the human condition in action! That's the grinding of the soul that makes for great literature! That's the chemistry of the soul!"* Because I knew, I simply *knew* that the lighthouse keeper was going to put his soul through the grinding mill of life if he chose against his gut feeling, and he was going to suffer just as Ernest Hemingway suffered for choosing to go against his better nature when he chose to betray his loving wife Hadley for his seductive, inveigling lover Pauline Pfeiffer.

"Thus conscience does make cowards of us all," said Shakespeare; but why? Why would conscience, man's moral center and guiding star, make cowards of us all if not for the onerous responsibility that goes with making a decision that conscience demands of us?

Hemingway's conscience demanded of him the moral imperative to be true to his wife Hadley, which meant that he would have to fight off his sexual/romantic attraction for Pauline Pfeiffer; but he couldn't. He wanted it all, and he was too weak to fight off his attraction.

That's what made the budding young writer, who would one day win the Nobel Prize for Literature, a coward. Ironically, his moral cowardice caused the fatal wound in his soul that gave him the *daimonic* fuel for some of his best stories; that's what I meant by the "chemistry of the soul," because Hemingway's fatal wound ground his soul from lover to lover until he could bear himself no longer and he killed himself, and I knew that the lighthouse keeper Tom Sherbourne would put his soul through the same grinding mill if he capitulated to his grieving wife's desire to keep the infant child that they had found in the boat with her dead father that had washed up on the shore of Janus

Island in Western Australia where he was the lighthouse keeper; he knew in his gut that they should seek out the infant child's birth mother, but they didn't, and that decision came back to haunt them, a story that made for a great novel by M. L. Stedman which became a great movie by the same title, *The Light Between Oceans*.

Ernest Hemingway left his wife for his lover, and that decision haunted him for the rest of his life, which he sadly owned up to in his bitter/sweet memoir *A Moveable Feast* that he was still working on just before taking his own life with his favorite bird shotgun at his home in Ketchum, Idaho: *"When I saw my wife again standing by the tracks as the train came in by the piled logs at the station, I wish I had died before I ever loved anyone but her."* He was reflecting on the decision he made to leave Hadley for Pauline, and he regretted it so much that he would rather have died had he known what his moral cowardice would do to him.

I watched *The Light Between Oceans* with anxious anticipation, because I *knew* that once Tom Sherbourne and his wife Isabel decided to keep the infant child and raise it as their own instead of notifying the authorities that one day life would call them to account for their moral transgression; and that's what I meant by "chemistry of the soul," which is a poetic way of saying that life has a way of grinding down the moral grist of one's soul, and I was no less angry at the lighthouse keeper for not being true to his conscience as I was for my high school hero and literary mentor Ernest Hemingway for betraying his faithful, loving wife Hadley for his calculating, seductive lover Pauline Pfeiffer. But then, where would we get our great literature from if not for the moral grinding of our soul?

29. Hemingway's Brain

Sunday, April 30, 2017

I should have anticipated it. That's why I wasn't taken by surprise when I read the piece by Joseph Brean on Hemingway's brain in yesterday's paper (*National Post, April 29, 2017*): "Head trauma linked to Hemingway's suicide." Medical science to the rescue…

Andrew Farah, chief of psychiatry at High Point Regional Health System at the University of North Carolina in Chapel Hill, wrote *Hemingway's Brain* in which he argues that the Nobel laureate's famous shotgun suicide in Ketchum, Idaho was the result of "chronic traumatic encephalopathy, the brain disease caused by repeated blows to the head," stating his case on his study of Hemingway's medical records, biographies on his life, and comparing Hemingway's early writing with his later writing, especially *A Movable Feast* which was the last thing he was working on before committing suicide shortly after being released from the Mayo Clinic where he had received electroshock therapy for manic depression.

Psychiatrist Andrew Farah focussed on Hemingway's nine major head traumas that he received throughout his life, the first one sustained in Italy during the First World War and the others in different accidents—car crash in London, skylight in Paris accidently falling on his head when he pulled the wrong chord, a fall on a fishing boat in the Gulf Coast, a plane crash in East Africa, and others which Farah argues were responsible for Hemingway's brain disease medically defined as chronic traumatic encephalopathy, or CTE.

"We all think of the Hemingway persona, but what the CTE did, later in life, was it simply solidified and locked in the very worst aspects of that persona. It made him irritable, volatile, difficult, and challenging," Farah said in an interview. "People talk about how, psychologically, he was trapped by the persona like a spy out too long, believing his own cover, or acting that way because people expected it of him. I think he was biologically incapable of breaking free from the nastier aspects of that persona, simply because of the CTE," Farah added, convinced in his belief of Hemingway's psychological condition.

Farah argues that the electroconvulsive therapy that Hemingway received at the Mayo Clinic for his severe depression and paranoid behavior made Hemingway's condition worse instead of better and believes that Hemingway was misdiagnosed and should not have been given electroshock treatment, and he may be right; but it seems to me (I haven't read his book yet, but I've put it on my Amazon wish list) that he's trying to fit Hemingway's very complex psychological condition into his medical theory, and it smells bad to me.

Hemingway played with the idea of suicide all his life, often threatening to take his life to get his own way with his four wives, and he played out this theme of suicide in one of his earliest and most canonical stories, "A Clean, Well-Lighted Place," and according to his official biographer Carlos Baker while still working on his first novel *The Sun Also Rises* Hemingway wrote in one of his meditations on suicide: "When I feel low, I like to think about death and the various ways of dying. And I think about probably the best way, unless you could arrange to die some way while asleep, would be to go off a liner at night." But his love of life always overrode his death wish and he survived until he could no longer live life on his own terms; so I have grave doubts about Farah's theory of Hemingway's famous suicide.

But what intrigues me about Farah's theory is that he believes the dark side of Hemingway's personality was "solidified" and "locked in" by Hemingway's deteriorating brain disease caused by traumatic head injuries. Why the dark and ugly side of Hemingway's personality and not the better side of his nature? Curious, what?

Were the novelists Robert Louis Stevenson (*The Strange Case of Dr. Jekyll and Mr. Hyde*), Dostoevsky (*The Double*), and Oscar Wilde *(The Picture of Dorian Gray)* wrong in their psychological take on the dual nature of the human personality? Why does medical science want to relegate the self of man to the brain and reduce man's behavior to biology and the dustbin of medical waste when the body dies? Have we become *this* materialistic?

There's so much more to Hemingway's suicide than the good psychiatrist can see, and though there's evidence to support the theory that traumatic brain injury can cause changes to one's personality, it does not discount the ancient belief in the dual nature of human consciousness that poets have written about for centuries; and if I were to offer my opinion on Hemingway's CTE, I'd be inclined to say that his behavior was more psychologically affected than neurologically induced. "That's the way we Hemingways are. We're nice guys one day and sons-of-bitches the next," said Hemingway's son Jack, who never suffered from CTE; but his model/actress daughter Margaux Hemingway committed suicide. It's probably in the genes, then; but that's another theory...

30. My Parents' Influence on My Writing Life

Monday, May 1, 2017

I've written very little about my parents, less about my mother than my father (he inspired my story "Enantiodromia," not yet published, and I wrote a poem on my mother that my young brother read at her funeral service which I did not attend), because I've never wanted to go there; but yesterday it was raining heavily and I listened to Eleanor Wachtel on *Writers & Company* on CBC radio interviewing Paula Fox on her memoir *Borrowed Finery,* and Fox's disarmingly frank revelations about her "sociopathic" mother and alcoholic father gave me licence to say something about my parents' influence on my writing life.

By no stretch of the imagination was my mother sociopathic. If anything, she was a very proud and good Roman Catholic Calabrian peasant wife and mother who immigrated to Canada to make a better life for her family, and my father was also a good man who became a closet alcoholic because he could not cope with the language and harsh reality of life in a foreign country, and what made my parents relevant to my literary life was the dynamic of their contentious relationship which took me years to come to terms with and which had an enormous influence upon my writing life because it affected me more than I realized.

As I listened to Paula Fox read excerpts from her memoir, I was arrested by the structure of her sentences, so compact and comprehensive that they sounded like a story in themselves, and I couldn't get over the effect they had upon me. They sounded better and truer than Hemingway's true sentences, and I had to sit back and wonder at the individual genius of the writer's talent that reflects the reality of their personal path.

At one point in the interview Paula Fox said to Eleanor Wachtel, who has a special gift for interviewing writers, *"I think you make the path as you walk,"* which confirmed the reality of my own journey of self-discovery and, upon reflection, the contentious nature of my parents' relationship; and then Paula Fox said something else that spoke to me personally and to the creative process of self-individuation: *"A lie hides the truth and a story tries to find it out,"* which was why I wrote so little about my mother and father in my fiction.

I could never understand why I was born into my family, I was so different; and upon reading Jess Stearn's book *The Search for the Soul: The Psychic Lives of Taylor Caldwell* in my early twenties, I knew that one day I would have my own past-life regressions to find out what my karmic relationship was with my mother and father and siblings, and which I did when Penny and I moved to Georgian Bay many years later.

I had to find out the cause of my parents' contentious relationship, and in my first past-life regression I went back to my most immediate past lifetime and learned that my mother, myself, and all my siblings were members of the British aristocracy in the mid 19th Century, but not my father; he was a member of the common class in that lifetime.

So there it was: the elitism and arrogance of my mother's immediate past lifetime pushing up through the subconscious and seeping into the mind of a proud Roman Catholic southern Italian illiterate peasant woman to create a paradoxical personality that was always at inexplicable odds with my father who could never win with my mother no matter what he did because it was never good enough for her, though she loved him, and I tell this story in my novel *Cathedral of My Past Lives* that I have not yet published because it's too personal.

I have written about my parents, then; but obliquely. And if I do write about them, it will probably be in bits and pieces in short fiction. That's the only way I will ever get rid of that lump of painful truth pushing at my heart and do justice to my mother and father who taught me more about the shadow side of human nature than anyone else, including Jung who gave me the language to understand the influence my parents had upon my writing life…

Just for the record though, because I don't believe I have ever included in any of my books my eulogy poem on my mother that my young brother read at her funeral service which I did not attend, I'd like to quote it in this journal on my writing life; it is, after all, the most private thing that I have said and probably will ever say about my mother: —

Ciao Mom, I Love You

Now that Mom has gone to the Other Side,
I feel an emptiness I have never known before.

From life to life to life,
I came into this world to look for my way back home to God,
and in Mother's aching heart I found my true self.

Not a day will go by when I will not think of her love,
her special blessing of peace and joy;
but I respect her choice to say goodbye,
and gracefully exist this painful world.

I dreamt of Dad a few days before Mom's passing,
and I knew he had come to take her home;
not for the first time, nor the second,
so great was their bond of human love.
And now together again, they can plan their destined end,
and fulfill God's Great Design.

I thank you Mom and Dad, for this, my precious life;
and for my brothers and sisters who made my life so true,
and for all the times we shared,
me being me, and you being you.

Now Mother, it's time to let go and say goodbye;
and though we all cry for you,
we know that your special love for us will never die.

Ciao Mom, I love you.

31. Why Hemingway, Anyway?

Tuesday, May 2, 2017

After I saw Penny off to work this morning I was going to go back upstairs to read what I had written earlier, but I looked at the books piled on the right side of the first four steps of our staircase that I had amassed there from last summer and this past month for outside reading on the front deck, and I felt nudged to dip into *The Essential Rumi* by Coleman Barks, and opening the book to where I had left off (I leave book markers in all the books I'm reading) my eyes fell upon the words I had highlighted from the poem "A Thirsty Fish," and I knew instantly why I had been nudged to read Rumi this morning: **"I have a thirsty fish in me /that can never find enough /of what it's thirsty for!"**

"That's Hemingway!" I exclaimed to myself, excited by the Sufi poet's insight into the deepest need of the insatiable writer's life, to be the greatest writer of his generation; and then I read the lines I had highlighted in the same bright orange color of the next poem "Enough Words?" and I could not believe how serendipity had once again provided me with a poetic insight into the essential nature of Hemingway's character: **"No matter how fast you run, /your shadow more than keeps up. /Sometimes, it's in front!"**

"Wow!" I exclaimed again, incredulous of my find; and I knew that I had my entry into the thought that had possessed me once again about coming back to Hemingway. I read the next six lines and I had the whole map of Hemingway's life: **"Only full, overhead sun /diminishes your shadow. /But that shadow has been serving you! /What hurts you, blesses you. Darkness is your candle. Your boundaries are your quest."**

This poetic insight into the pattern of Hemingway's whole life brought to mind a line from *Meeting the Shadow: The Hidden Power of the Dark Side of Human Nature*, edited by Connie Zweig and Jeremiah Abrams, and I took it off my shelf to look it up (I often remember the gist of lines I have highlighted): **"The shadow is both**

the awful thing that needs redemption, and the suffering redeemer who can provide it," --exactly what Rumi intuited in his poem, and I had all I needed to answer why I was called back to Hemingway again because Hemingway's shadow was both his curse and his blessing. But it's going to be very, very personal; and maybe that's the real reason I was called back to my high school hero and literary mentor…

Doctor Farah based his theory on Hemingway's suicide upon his belief that the injuries to Hemingway's brain brought about by blows to his head affected his sense of self, which may very well be true; but the self of man is not biologically based. It is spiritual in essence and pre-exists the body and will continue to exist after the body dies. This can't be proven according to the limits of scientific inquiry, so man's sense of self continues to be limited to his biology until science can prove otherwise. This is the flaw in Farah's argument on Hemingway's suicide, but I can't prove it just as he cannot prove that Hemingway's sense of self was not self-determined by the values he chose to live by. What's one to do, then?

I dropped out of university in my third year of philosophy studies because I feared drowning in a sea of endless speculation and decided to build my life upon the *terra firma* of my own experiences, which I did; and, to quote Paula Fox, I made my own path as I walked through life until I felt confident enough in the truth of my own experiences to trust my intuitive understanding of the self of man to be spiritual in essence and not biologically based, which is why I have grave doubts about Farah's theory of Hemingway's suicide.

Hemingway had a nasty side to his personality (the cruelest man she knew, said his third wife Martha Gellhorn), and though he inherited his family's shadow personality traits, as we all do, he was primarily responsible for his own dark side by the values he chose to live by, which were fundamentally self-serving because he was driven by his *daimon* to become the greatest writer of his generation which made him single-minded and cruelly opportunistic; and by the time he won the Nobel Prize for Literature his shadow had autonomous power over his massive ego, which led Doctor Farah to conclude that the "nastier aspects of his persona" were "solidified" and "locked" into his personality, and though CTE (chronic traumatic encephalopathy) may have contributed to setting his shadow free, the reality of my own journey of self-discovery has convinced me that Hemingway's personality was shadow-afflicted from an early age and grew in proportion to his fame and success until it took over his personality completely and drove him deep into depression and suicide.

The shadow is by its nature the dark aspects of one's personality that one keeps repressed to the unconscious, but to realize wholeness and singleness of self, which is the destined purpose of man's existence (again, this isn't something one can prove; one has to be initiated into this mystery if one's path will allow it), one has to assimilate one's shadow with their conscious ego personality (this is what Jesus meant by making the two into one), and this is not an easy thing to do, which I can vouchsafe because I transcended myself by making my two selves into one and realized my true self which I've written about in *The Pearl of Great Price* and my twin soul books *Death, the Final Frontier* and *The Merciful Law of Divine Synchronicity*; but this is personal and not scientific, whatever that may mean, so I don't expect anyone to believe me. Why Hemingway, then?

Because he was my high school hero and literary mentor whose literary life provided me with the perfect analogue for my own shadow-afflicted life that I had to wrestle with on my excruciating journey of self-discovery, the difference being that my call to writing was superseded by my call to finding my true self and I did not place all of my eggs into one basket like Hemingway did, and I found my true self and Hemingway didn't.

This is why I've been called back to Hemingway, then; to shed more light upon the path to one's true self through Hemingway's shadow-afflicted personality...

32. Reading the Language of Life

Wednesday, May 3, 2017

It turns out that our goldfish Goober had something called swim bladder which was responsible for him twisting his body into a circle when I thought it was because he had outgrown his tank and needed more space to swim in, which may very well have been the case despite his swim bladder condition, but does that negate the message that I read into his behavior which I took to mean that I had to expand the parameters of my life?

The old soothsayers used to read the language of life in animal entrails and in the flight of birds and other natural events that to the average observer meant nothing, so what is this mystery of soothsaying that continues to mystify people?

Personally, I think it's a sixth sense, a higher type of knowing like extra-sensory perception, a highly intuitive gift which some people are born with; but it can be developed as one grows in their knowledge of how life works. Carl Jung, for example, practiced the ancient Chinese art of divination when he needed guidance; but he stopped using the I Ching method of divination when he had honed his instincts enough to trust his own judgment, just as I did when I stopped my own experiment of tossing a coin into the air to make up my mind for me, a technique that I called *"letting go and letting God."*

When my personal path took me as far as it could in my journey of self-discovery, I suffered unbearable anguish; and as always happened when I hit another wall, *the omniscient guiding principle of life* came to my assistance. In this case, I was given the inspiration to toss a coin into the air to make up my mind for me in the belief that I would be *"letting go and letting God,"* meaning I would place my absolute trust in *"divine chance."*

Heads I do, tails I don't. This was a very difficult stage on my journey of self-discovery, but I did not falter, and every difficult decision that I had to make I did so with the toss of a coin; but I had to be true to the toss or my experiment would have meant nothing.

I lost a possible romance because my toss told me not to pursue my interest in a young woman who had eyes for me, but in my gut I felt I should not pursue it and the toss confirmed it. And then I began to notice something. Whenever my gut feelings told me to go with a decision, the toss confirmed it; and whenever my gut feelings told me not to go with a decision, the toss confirmed it. *This happened with every single toss!* And that's when I realized that *"letting go and letting God"* merely meant trusting my own gut feelings; and I stopped tossing a coin to make up my mind for me and learned to trust my intuition.

I was glad to learn years later when I began reading Jung that he had forfeited the I Ching for his own intuitive judgement, but what we both learned from our respective intentions proved noteworthy: we all have superior insight which speaks to us through intuition, and the more we learn to trust our intuitive instincts the more in tune we will be with *the omniscient guiding principle of life.* This is what Jesus meant when he said that one must have ears to hear and eyes to see. He was speaking about our superior insight.

So when I saw our goldfish Goober's body twisted into a circle the thought came to me that he had "curled" in upon himself because his fish tank was too small, and Penny purchased a larger tank for him. He did straighten out for a few days, and then he circled in upon himself again; and then Penny went on Google and learned about swim bladder and we changed Goober's diet and his swim bladder condition was cured and he went back to normal. But does Goober's real condition of swim bladder negate the insight into my own condition which I read to mean that my personal parameters needed to be expanded?

No, I don't believe so; and I say this because over the years I've seen that it doesn't matter how one gets the message from *the omniscient guiding principle of life,* it's the message that counts. And I read the message from our goldfish Goober as a symbolic confirmation of my call back to Hemingway to concentrate on creative writing to expand my horizons, both literary and personal. But one could ask: how can you trust this message? After all, it's all in your mind; isn't it?

It is in my own mind, certainly; but I put myself through the test of *"letting go and letting God"* with my outrageous experiment of tossing a coin into the air to let "chance" make up my mind for me, and I learned from this experience to trust my own gut feelings; so when I got the call to go back to Hemingway with the Christmas gift of an *Indigo Hemingway Notebook* from Penny's sister, I trusted the message to expand my creative horizons, and the message that I got from our goldfish Goober confirmed it...

33. Hemingway's Prison

Friday, May 5, 2017

Hemingway trapped himself. He became a prisoner of his own personality, which had become so shadow-afflicted by all of his betrayals and self-betrayals that it drove him to suicide. He told his young friend Aaron Hotchner that if he couldn't live life on his own terms there was no point in living it, and he was true to himself.

But which self was he true to, his real or false self? That was his dilemma. As Sartre, who visited Hemingway at his home the *Finca Vigia* in Cuba and appreciated Hemingway for his stories that gave flesh to his no-exit philosophy, would say: *he was what he was not, and he was not what he was.* Hemingway was torn between his *being* and *non-being*, the two selves of his personality; or, as Gurdjieff would say, he stood between two chairs.

So I was called back to Hemingway again because I had more to say about his path which I explored in *The Lion that Swallowed Hemingway,* a path that brought him world fame and adulation but which did so much damage to his soul that it destroyed him; and as presumptuous as this may seem, given all the writers and scholars and now a psychiatrist that have written on his life and writing, my intimate familiarity with the archetypal shadow personality gives me all the gnostic certainty that I need to write a sequel to *The Lion that Swallowed Hemingway,* which is what this journal has turned out to be.

I've often wondered what it was about Hemingway that attracted me in the first place, other than the romantic lure of his adventurous life which I could never emulate because I was called to a higher path of self-discovery, but when I had that eureka moment watching *Hemingway and Gellhorn* on TV three years ago and saw the *enantiodromiac paradox* of his shadow-afflicted personality, I knew why I had been called to Hemingway in high school—because his *daimonic* drive to become the greatest writer of his generation was no less fierce than my own *daimonic* drive to find my true self, and our two paths collided when I saw the tragic limitations of Hemingway's inability to resolve his conflicted nature in the movie based upon his tempestuous relationship with his third wife who called him a pathological liar.

The *enantiodromiac paradox* of Hemingway's life was his inability to make his two selves into one, despite his best efforts to do so through the integrative process of writing which, as every writer knows (either intuitively and/or cognitively), blends and melds and fuses the fragmented aspects of one's ego/shadow personality into one whole self.

"All you know is yourself, if you know yourself," said Paula Fox in Aida Edemarian's feature article "A Qualified Optimist" in *The Guardian*. "But there's something about the process of writing that refines all the elements so they don't bear the stamp of personality. They're intensely personal, but they are also extra-personal. I think probably there isn't any catharsis possible. You get a sense of order from arranging things. *It's a process of growth, of wisdom and spirit*. Those are big words, but...*in a sense you become a different person after you have written them.* So perhaps that's catharsis—becoming different, not becoming better or worse," Paula Fox said, confirming what Hemingway felt about writing through which he worked out in his stories and novels the emotional conflicts that haunted him, like his love/hate relationship with his father and deep-seated animus for his "bitch" of a mother and unrequited love for nurse Agnes von Kurowsky and the young Adriana Ivancich.

Hemingway was much more sensitive than most creative writers, and his feelings for people affected him deeply; but beneath his charming exterior ran a vicious streak of cruelty that he worked out in his writing, like his portrait of his friend Harold Loeb who became the contemptable Robert Cohn in *The Sun Also Rises,* and his composite portrait of his mother and wife Pauline Pfeiffer and lover Jane Mason in Macomber's wife in "The Short Happy Life of Francis Macomber," or the compromised writer Harry in "The Snows of Kilimanjaro" who was brilliantly inspired by his friend Scott Fitzgerald who recommended Hemingway to his editor Maxwell Perkins who launched Hemingway's career with *The Sun Also Rises.*

But writing was Hemingway's calling to his real self, and by working out his emotional conflicts and ontological impasses in his stories and novels he had some measure of control over his paradoxical personality which puzzled everyone who knew him. "He was so complicated, so many sides to him you could hardly make a sketch of him in a geometry book," said his first wife Hadley Richardson; and in his book *Dance of the Chameleons* Truman Capote called Hemingway "a closet everything," which spoke to more than Hemingway's private sexual desires that he also tried to work out in his writing.

"He was a complex, very difficult man with a tremendous zest for life and when he did anything he did it absolutely up to the hilt, no half measures," said Thomas Shevlin to Denis Brian in his book *The True Gen*, but it was this tremendous zest for life with a no half measure imperative that trapped Hemingway in the prison of his ego/shadow personality, and so trapped was he that he could no longer bear what he had become and killed himself; and whether this was tragic or heroic one cannot say because, after all, it was Hemingway. As Denis Brian concluded his intimate portrait of Hemingway by those who knew him: "I now believe they (his falsehoods, betrayals and self-betrayals) fueled Hemingway's superman alter ego, a self-deception he needed in order to survive. A remarkable man still emerges, one seen by some as diabolical and by others striving toward sainthood. What is beyond dispute is this: he suffered. He created. His art endures. And that's the true gen."

34. Hemingway's Out-of-body Experience

Sunday, May 7, 2017

In a letter to Bernard Berenson in 1954, Hemingway wrote: "You know that fiction, prose rather, is possibly the toughest trade of all in writing. You do not have the reference, the old important reference. You have the sheet of blank paper, the pencil, and the obligation to invent truer than things can be true. You have to take what is not palpable and make it completely palpable and also have it seem normal and so that it can become a part of the experience of the person who reads it" (*Selected Letters*, p. 837).

Eighteen-year-old Ernest Hemingway got badly wounded in WW 1 when he was an ambulance driver for the American Red Cross in Italy. He was delivering cigarettes and candy bars to soldiers on the front when a mortar shell exploded and shattered his leg with shrapnel, and he had an out-of-body experience. He rose out of his body and saw his body below him and thought he was dead. This was not an ordinary experience, but he wrote about it in a short story and in his novel *A Farewell to Arms*, and it was palpable enough to be "truer than true."

In his story "Now I Lay Me," Nick Adams, Hemingway's fictional self, is back home from the war, but the effects of the war still haunt him: "I myself did not want to sleep because I had been living for a long time with the knowledge that if I ever shut my eyes in the dark and let myself go, my soul would get out of my body. I had been that way for a long time, ever since I had been blown up at night and felt it go out of me and go off and then come back. I tried never to think about it, but it had started to go since, in the night, just at the moment of going off to sleep, and I could only stop it by a very great effort. So while now I am fairly sure it would not really have gone out, yet then, that summer, I was unwilling to make the experiment." So it happened more than once, then.

Not everyone has an out-of-body experience, and people who do have them don't want to talk about them because they don't want to appear strange; but Hemingway gave his out-of-body experience a context that made it palpable. I had an out-of-body experience also when I had open-heart surgery, but when I mentioned this to my surgeon he got the most startled look on his face and excused himself as quickly as possible.

Obviously, he didn't want to go there; but going there is what my writing is all about, and by "there" I mean the reality of my journey of self-discovery, a state of consciousness that allowed and continues to allow for non-ordinary states of consciousness that have taken all of my creative efforts to make palpable in books like *The Lion that Swallowed Hemingway*, and especially in *The Pearl of Great Price* and *The Merciful Law of Divine Synchronicity.*

This is why I've come to believe that I'm writing for posterity, because I don't think today's reader is ready to read about the archetypal journey of soul's evolution through life embodied in a real person like myself; it's too much to swallow. It's much more credible when written as allegory, like *The Conference of the Birds* by the mystic Sufi poet Attar, or Paulo Coelho's simple adventure/fantasy novel *The Alchemist* that even people like President Clinton and actress Julia Roberts read and helped make so popular that it sold over sixty million copies throughout the world; but I write and write because I love the joy of discovery that writing gives me. And so did Hemingway who, like all creative writers, couldn't wait to see how his stories turned out; but only Hemingway had the wisdom of his formative years as a hard-nosed journalist to keep his stories existentially grounded, despite his out-of-body experience which he made palpable enough to believe.

This is my challenge, then. This is why I was called back to Hemingway with Penny's sister's serendipitous gift of the *Indigo Hemingway Notebook,* to write fictional stories about my own life like Hemingway wrote about his (the more I read and study Hemingway this time around, the more I see just how autobiographical his stories and novels really are), and it's my challenge to make palpable my impalpable journey of self-discovery just as Hemingway made palpable his out-of-body experience, not to mention his androgynous sexual desires that are much less shocking today than they were in Hemingway's day, which was why his novel *The Garden of Eden* was published posthumously.

How I'm going to do this, I don't know; but I've never not trusted my Muse before, and I don't intend to start now. *"December, 2016. Orest, a place for your stories to begin. Merry Christmas,"* wrote Penny's sister in my *Indigo Hemingway Notebook*; and from the day I received Melanie's gift, I've been taking notes for my new stories…

35. Hemingway's Way

Monday, May 8, 2017

I'm half way through another reading of *Ernest Hemingway: A Life Story*, by Carlos Baker, and when I stopped to rest my eyes this morning after several hours of reading the phrase "the heart of the matter" popped into my mind, and I knew I could no longer put it off; and so, once again into the breach of my writing life...

I did my utmost to give expression to the secret way, the mystical path to wholeness and completeness, in my book *The Merciful Law of Divine Synchronicity*, which was best expressed in my spiritual musing "The Purpose of Art is Art's Purpose" that I quoted in Chapter 6, "The Eye of the Needle," and I know that the imperative of my call back to Hemingway is to give expression to the secret way in the stories I keep putting off writing because they're too close to home, and I have taken down a number of titles for these stories in my *Hemingway Notebook* that I look forward with excited trepidation to writing, but until I make a definite connection between the secret way and creative writing I will never get to the heart of the matter, and by this I mean the driving force of Hemingway's life.

I've been reading so much Hemingway these past few months that I'm starting to get sick of Hemingway. He was a very nasty man. Selfish, cruel, vindictive, and unforgiving to those who hurt or slighted him in any way; but he had a genius for writing, which he cultivated with an industry that writers envied as he tells us in *A Moveable Feast*, and it's this genius that interests me as I delve deeper into the secret way of literature that Hemingway brought to aesthetic fruition in many stories, especially *The Old Man and the Sea* that brought the paradoxical nature of Hemingway's life as close to artistic resolution as he could take it.

My breakthrough insight into Hemingway's life came with the movie *Hemingway and Gellhorn,* which played out the tempestuous dynamic of their relationship, a testament to Clive Owen who played

Ernest Hemingway and Nicole Kidman who played Martha Gellhorn, because in the bitter, angry, and resentful give-and-take of their separate needs I saw the *enantiodromiac* play of the human personality, which is why I shouted (to the surprise of Penny and our dinner guests): *"That's it! He had to have that to become a great writer! Hemingway had to be a prick to become the great writer that he became!"*

What I saw in that moment of heightened awareness was Hemingway's ego/shadow personality, the two sides of his paradoxical nature fused into one, and for the first time in my study of the individuation process of the man's nature I finally caught a glimpse of the *enantiodromiac* dynamic of the human personality in Hemingway as he fought and argued with his wife Martha Gellhorn who refused to buckle to her husband's selfish needs because she too was *daimonically* driven to realize her own identity as a writer, and that's what set free my book *The Lion that Swallowed Hemingway*, the lion being Hemingway's shadow.

"How do you find a lion that has swallowed you?" asked Carl Jung, I imagine with a twinkle in his venerable octogenarian eyes; and in my euphoric insight into Hemingway's life I saw the lion that had swallowed Hemingway but which he was willfully blind to—except in his writing which demanded total honesty to his artistic credo; that's why I shouted that he had to be a prick to become the great writer that he became...

The *enantiodromiac* dynamic of the human personality is the constant play of one's ego personality with one's shadow (one's *being* and *non-being*), a play that can never be resolved by the natural process of individuation because to resolve the paradoxical nature of one's evolving self-consciousness one has to take evolution into their own hands and live by values that transform and transcend one's ego/shadow personality, which is not an easy thing to do because it goes against man's primal selfish nature. And this is the mystery that stumps most writers and seekers, especially writers who become seekers like Thomas Wolfe.

Man is by instinct a selfish creature. This is his primordial nature, and despite all the tempering forces of an evolving social consciousness man is fundamentally selfish at the core and cannot and will not realize wholeness and singleness of self, which Jesus called making the two into one, until he curbs his selfish nature and learns to transcend himself. This is the paradoxical reality of our *becoming*, which took me a lifetime to work out.

In his novel *You Can't Go Home Again,* Thomas Wolfe—the most voluminous writer that his editor Maxwell Perkins had ever worked with, Wolfe carting his manuscripts into Max's office in crates laden with thousands of hand-written pages—George, Wolfe's alter ego, shouts to his friend Randy: "No, that's not what bothers me. The thing I've got to find out is the way! The *way!* The *way!* Do you understand?"

"George's face was full of perplexity," Wolfe writes. "He was silent, trying to phrase the problem." And Wolfe continues, phrasing George's problem*: "I'm looking for the way,"* he said at last. "I think it may be something like what people vaguely mean when they speak of fiction. *A kind of legend, perhaps. Something—a story—composed of all the knowledge I have, all of the living I've seen.* Not the facts, you understand—not just the record of my life—but something truer than the facts—something distilled out of my experience and transmitted into a form of universal application. That's what the best fiction is, isn't it?" (*You Can't Go Home Again,* by Thomas Wolfe, p. 330, Italics mine.)

In one brilliant sentence, Thomas Wolfe captured the entire aesthetic of Hemingway's *way*: "Not the facts, you understand—not just the record of my life—but something truer than the facts—something distilled out of my experience and transmitted into a form of universal application," which Wolfe called "the best of fiction." That's what Hemingway was after with his "one true sentence" principle. "All good books are alike in that they are truer than if they had really happened," he wrote in *By-Line: Ernest Hemingway,* which he proved with creative genius in "The Short Happy Life of Francis Macomber" and "The Snows of Kilimanjaro" in which he distilled the facts of his African safari into an experience truer than the facts; which, in the dialectical process of creative writing, transcended the facts and became art.

That's Hemingway's *way* and the heart of the matter; and that's why I was called back to him, so I can distill the secret way out of my own experiences and transmute them into "a universal form of application," which was Wolfe's metaphor for the sacred knowledge of the secret way that was too elusive for him to grasp. And that's the irony of Thomas Wolfe's life, as it was for Hemingway and every creative writer, because the secret way to wholeness and singleness of self reveals itself through the creative process of writing.

But, as Katherine Mansfield came to realize to her infinite regret, writing was not enough to satisfy the longing in her soul to be what she was meant to be, and she sought a teaching that would satisfy her deepest longing, which she found in Gurdjieff like I did when serendipity placed Ouspensky's book *In Search of the Miraculous* into my hands; and when I write the stories that I'm called upon to write, unlike Thomas Wolfe and my high school hero and literary mentor, I will do so cognizant of the secret way of literature...

36. Hemingway's Writing Vocabulary

Tuesday, May 9. 2017

I don't remember where I read it, but scholars made a study of Ernest Hemingway's writing vocabulary and determined that it was limited to 900 words, and according to Professor Harold Bloom who wrote *Shakespeare: The Invention of the Human,* William Shakespeare's writing vocabulary was more than 21000 words, 20100 words more than Hemingway's deliberately circumscribed vocabulary, a difference that leads one to wonder about the creative process—be it poetry, short stories, novels, plays, or discursive essays.

Hemingway's uncle helped him get a job for the *Kansas City Star* where as an eighteen year-old cub reporter he was trained to write short simple sentences, and during his apprenticeship years in Paris where he picked up invaluable advice on writing from Ezra Pound, Gertrude Stein, James Joyce, Ford Maddox Ford, Scott Fitzgerald and every writer whom he felt had something to teach him, including Sherwood Anderson who advised Hemingway and his wife Hadley to go to Paris instead of Italy where Ernest wanted to go, providing Hemingway with letters of introduction to Gertrude Stein and other writers and Sylvia Beach who owned the bookstore and lending library *Shakespeare & Company* to help break the ice for him but whom he later betrayed by satirizing Anderson's style in his vicious parody *The Torrents of Spring* to get out of a contract with his publisher, Hemingway forged a style of his own which he founded upon his "one true sentence" principle, always telling his story "the way it was" which he heightened with his fertile imagination, a technique that he deduced from studying Cezanne's paintings, a condensed "cablese" style of writing that was so reader friendly that he appealed to all readers, the unsophisticated who lacked the learning of a higher education and the more sophisticated because his stories spoke to the human condition with existential depth and clarity; and that was Hemingway's mystique.

I remember sitting in the loft of our triplex unit that I was building in my hometown of Nipigon in Northwestern Ontario reading a paperback copy of Hemingway's book of short stories *Winner Take Nothing* when out of sheer frustration and resentment I threw the book against the wall. *"How in the hell did he become so famous writing such simple stories?"* I swore to myself, and it took a few more years before I broke through the mystique of Hemingway's deceptively simple style and grew to appreciate his writing.

I did a lot of reading and writing before I learned that just because Hemingway was easy to read did not mean that his stories were simple, and it took a few more years before I realized that Hemingway's style was much too constraining for me and I had to write in a style that gave me more freedom, a more expansive style like Joyce's *Dubliners* and *A Portrait of the Artist as a Young Man* that I read in high school but whose novel *Ulysses* I could never finish because Joyce went to the opposite extreme from Hemingway's plain and simple style, and I had to find a style of my own between those polar opposites.

Words. It's all about words, and if you don't have the right words to express the nuances of thought and feeling how can one write not a good, better, but best story?

As I've already said in one of my journal entries, William Faulkner, with whom Hemingway had a contentious relationship (he bitterly resented Faulkner for getting the Nobel Prize before him), accused Hemingway of being afraid to use big words, and Hemingway replied that he didn't need big words to express big emotions, and he was right. His stories were full of big emotions, and I loved his stories (except his novel *Across the River and into the Trees*, but I may change my mind in my re-reading now that I know so much more about Hemingway's private life and feelings); but regardless how much he appealed to me, I always felt there was something missing in Hemingway's style that vexed me, and it took a few more years to figure out what I felt was missing but which I found in other writers.

Once I figured out how Hemingway packed his stories with meaning, using his now-famous ice-berg theory and other clever techniques that crafted his stories into art, I got the uneasy but excited feeling that for all of his appeal Hemingway was cheating, and it wasn't until I discovered the preternaturally gifted literary critic Professor Harold Bloom that I figured out what it was about Hemingway's writing that bothered me, and it was Bloom's book *Shakespeare: The Invention of the Human* that gave me the clue.

"Shakespeare's vocabulary remains extraordinary in the history of highly imaginative literature: more than twenty-one thousand words, eighteen hundred of which he coined," said Professor Bloom in the introduction of his book *The Shadow of a Great Rock: Literary Appreciation of the King James Bible,* which holds to a mere eight thousand words. "The richness of Shakespeare's language gives a very different effect from that of the KJB (and Ernest Hemingway). At once opulent and elliptical, Shakespeare's cognitive music is unique in literature," wrote Professor Bloom, but Hemingway preferred to write plain and simple like the King James Bible and not like the bard William Shakespeare; that's what made him so appealing to both sophisticated and unsophisticated readers.

But not everyone liked Hemingway's simple style, especially writers like Pat Conroy whose model was Thomas Wolfe. Just sixteen when introduced to Wolfe by his English teacher Eugene Norris, Conroy devoured Wolfe's novel *Look Homeward, Angel* and couldn't get enough of Wolfe's writing; but seeing the powerful effect that Wolfe's effusive style was having on his impressionable student, Norris introduced the fledgling writer to Hemingway's spare novel *The Old Man and the Sea* to temper his impassioned spirit. But it was too late.

Wolfe had already inflicted an immortal wound upon young Pat Conroy's soul, and many years later in his introduction to an anniversary edition of Wolfe's novel *Of Time and the River*, he tells us why. "Elegant concision with language would never be one of my anxieties," wrote the author of *The Great Santini*. "The cool hard sentences of Hemingway were spare and shapely, but his sentences were trays of ice to me. I never could enroll in that it-is-true-and-good-and-spare-and-fine-and the road is dusty-school of American writing. The language genie found itself trapped in the bottle of my deepest self. It's language and its roaring sounded in my bloodstream and all my sentences began to look funny. I could not help it. Thomas Wolfe had led me by the hand and introduced me to myself." And if I'm truly honest with myself, that's the same effect that Hemingway's writing began to have on me; but with the difference that I now felt he was cheating by keeping it plain and simple.

Gene Norris gave Pat Conroy an invaluable piece of information when he brought young Pat to visit the boarding house in Asheville, North Carolina where Thomas Wolfe had grown up and written about in his novel *Look Homeward, Angel*, and after touring the house which deeply affected the impressionable boy they went into the back yard where the apples were beginning to ripen on a tree, North Carolina apples that his idol Thomas Wolfe claimed to be the best apples in the world. Norris leaped up and grabbed an apple from a low-lying branch and gave it to his student, commanding, "Eat it, boy."

Later in the car on the way out of Asheville, Pat asked his teacher, "Why'd you want me to eat the apple, Mr. Norris?" And Mr. Norris, in his great wisdom, replied: *"It's high time, boy, that you learned that there IS a relationship between life and art,"* implying of course that Thomas Wolfe's fiction was drawn entirely from his own life, as was Earnest Hemingway's and all writers of enduring literary fiction, as Pat Conroy was to prove with some of the most harrowing autobiographical novels in the annals of American literature—*The Great Santini*, *The Lords of Discipline,* and *The Prince of Tides* to name three.

All great writers know this instinctively, especially Thomas Wolfe and Ernest Hemingway who could not get enough of life to satisfy the irrepressible longing in their soul to be all they craved to be, and they lusted for all the life they could get which they then poured into their writing each according to their own style, Wolfe with Dionysian effusion and Hemingway with Spartan restraint, and though worlds apart in their styles they both were consumed by the sacred flame of literature which Wolfe called the *"way"* and Hemingway called "the secret that is poetry written into prose," but neither could explain it.

"A great style is itself necessarily a trope, a metaphor for a particular attitude towards life," wrote Professor Bloom in *Novelists and Novels.* "Hemingway's is an art of evocation, hardly a singular or original mode, except that Hemingway evokes by parataxis, in a manner of Whitman, or much in the English Bible" (which Hemingway boasted he read from cover to cover every year of his life, which I doubt very much because it was to his nature to hyperbolize; that's why his third wife called him an apocryphiar); but as evocative as his style was, it was missing something that gave me the uncomfortable feeling that he was cheating, and in a way I agreed with Hemingway's rival William Faulkner.

In *More Matter: Essays and Criticism*, John Updike reviewed *The Stories of Vladimir Nabokov* and had this to say about Nabokov's style: "What startling beauty of phrase, twists of thought, depths of sorrow, and bursts of wit! This was a rainbow prose that made most others look flat and gray." Evocative no less than Hemingway's style, but much richer in its evocation. "Nabokov was a kind of late Wordsworthian Romantic, ascribing a metaphysical meaning to the bliss that reality inspired in him...The mind in its shimmering workings provided his topic and permeated his narrative manner," wrote Updike, and that's what I felt was missing from Hemingway's style, the luxuriant texture of man's complex nature.

"The art of ellipsis, or leaving things out, indeed is the great virtue of Hemingway's best short stories," wrote Professor Bloom; but his laconic style bore too much weight for the story and gave me the feeling that he was cheating, a clever technique that had its limits but which inevitably invoked parody (and by Hemingway himself), because only so much reality can be expressed laconically, like trying to pour more into a container than it can hold. "I never could enroll in that it-is-true-and-good-and-spare-and-fine-and the road is dusty-school of American writing," said Pat Conroy, making the point about Hemingway's style.

This is what Professor Bloom meant by the premise of his book *Shakespeare: The Invention of the Human*. Shakespeare took in all of human nature, the physical and the metaphysical, and gave it expression with all the words he knew, and even had to invent eighteen hundred new words because man's nature is so complex; that's why I began to get the uneasy feeling that Hemingway was cheating and afraid to use big words.

It may not take big words to express big emotions, but it takes more than 900 words to draw an aesthetically satisfying image of the multifaceted soul of man. Hemingway always said that he wanted to write like Cezanne painted, but I'm not so sure now that he succeeded, and in his heart of hearts I'm inclined to believe that Hemingway knew this.

"Writing is something that you can never do as well as it can be done. It is a perpetual challenge and it is more difficult than anything else that I have ever done—so I do it. And it makes me happy when I do it well," he wrote in a letter to Ivan Kashkin in 1935, and he did write some amazing stories; but for all of his creative genius, I'm beginning to wonder now what all the fuss was about. But maybe, just maybe, this may be the deeper reason why I was called back to Hemingway, to take the shine off my high school hero and literary mentor and get on with my own stories that I keep putting off writing...

37. Founding Moments

I've been getting ideas for new stories ever since I got my *Hemingway Notebook* from Penny's sister, and all these new ideas have to do with an aspect of life that speak to what Alice Munro referred to as "something happened here" and which Miriam Toews called a *"founding moment,"* an event that affected one's life; and revealing the when, where, how, and why of the event IS the story. But why write about it? Something is always happening somewhere every moment of the day, but what is so special about a *"founding moment"* that is worthy of a story? That's what intrigues writers...

What happened? Where did it happen? Why did it happen? How did it happen? And what effect did it have upon those that it happened to? These are the elements of a good story, but what does it all mean? That's what writers try to work out through writing.

MEANING is what writers are after, the meaning of life through the events that happen to people. "It happened for a reason," people say, when they cannot fathom the why of an event (like cancer, a house fire, or accidental drowning of a child), but writers are not content with this; they have to know why something happened, even going so far as to invent a reason in their story or novel. This is what compelled Victor Frankl to write *Man's Search for Meaning*, and the answer that he worked out startled the world.

"What was really needed was a fundamental change in our attitude toward life," he wrote in his paradigm-shifting book drawn from his horrifying Nazi concentration camp experiences. "We had to learn ourselves and, furthermore, we had to teach the despairing men, that *it did not really matter what we expected from life, but rather what life expected of us.* We needed to stop asking about the meaning of life, and instead to think of ourselves as those who were being questioned by life—daily and hourly. Our answer must consist, not in talk or meditation, but in right action and right conduct. Life ultimately means taking the responsibility to find the right answer to its problems and to fulfill the tasks which it constantly sets for each individual" (*Man's Search for Meaning,* Victor Frankl, p. 98).

Albert Camus couldn't find the why of the Sisyphean struggle apart from the gods condemning Sisyphus to his hopeless fate (the deeper meaning of karmic accountability escaped the philosopher of the absurd), and he imagined Sisyphus happy rolling his rock up the hill for eternity because "the struggle itself towards the heights is enough to fill a man's heart." But I could never imagine Sisyphus happy, because there had to be a reason for man's daily struggle which the myth of Sisyphus symbolized; and in my journey of self-discovery I came to agree with Victor Frankl who dared to turn the question around and ask what life wanted of us, which gave him a whole new perspective on man's existence.

"Questions about the meaning of life can never be answered by sweeping statements. 'Life' does not mean something vague, but something very real and very concrete, just as life's tasks are also very real and concrete. They form man's destiny, which is different and unique for each individual. No man and no destiny can be compared with any other man or any other destiny. No situation repeats itself, and each situation calls for a different response," Frankl wrote in *Man's Search for Meaning,* which confirmed my own experience as I forged my own path through life by "working" on myself with Gurdjieff's teaching, my *Royal Dictum* (my edict of self-denial), and the sayings of Jesus; and although Frankl's existential paradigm did not embrace the larger perspective of reincarnation, it nonetheless confirmed that *man must work out the meaning of life through his response to life,* which is precisely what writers try to do with every story they write; and herein lies the mystery of what Wolfe called the "*way*" and Hemingway called "the secret that is poetry written into prose" and Emerson called the "God within" and I came to call *the omniscient guiding principle of life* and Norman Mailer called the "spooky art" that he couldn't fathom.

And it is spooky, as every writer who is honest with himself knows, because who can explain where ideas for a poem or a story come from? But that's the point, isn't it? That's why I'm committed to exploring my call back to Hemingway, to get to the bottom of this mysterious process that Mailer called "spooky" which I hope to do with my understanding of the secret way of life that I discovered in my long journey of self-discovery.

Hemingway never realized "wholeness and singleness of self," to use Jung's words, and he died a conflicted and tortured man; but why was he so conflicted? That's the question that stumps everyone, despite Doctor Andrew Farah's attempt to rationalize Hemingway's bi-polar mood swings and suicidal personality, because there's much more to the self than neuropsychiatry can explain. As Rumi said in one of his poems: *"These leaves, our bodily personalities, seem identical, /but the globe of soul fruit /we make, /each is elaborately /unique,"* telling us that there is more to the personality than we can see.

Rumi tells us in his cryptic way that through the daily growth of our personality we "make" our own soul, what he called a "globe of soul fruit," which was the premise of Gurdjieff's self-transformative teaching because he believed that man is not born with an immortal soul but can create one if he knows how, and despite Gurdjieff's misperception of man's essential nature, his teaching helped one to realize their immortal self. This was the premise of my book *Gurdjieff Was Wrong But His Teaching Works.*

And this is what inspired my spiritual musing "The Prison of Personality," because if we create a personality that traps our immortal soul we will never transcend ourselves and realize wholeness and singleness of self; and the solution to man's dilemma is the mystical art of self-reconciliation, which Jung explored in his psychology of individuation that he developed from his profoundly in-depth studies of ancient Gnostic and alchemical texts and his own "confrontation with the unconscious" that he chronicled in his very private journal *The Red Book;* but what does this have to do with the spooky art of writing? What does the creative process have to do with the individuation process and self-realization?

That's what writers cannot fathom. But some writers *do* fathom the mystery, writers like the Sufi poet Rumi and Emily Dickinson; but not Hemingway, because like the rich young man in Christ's parable Hemingway wanted to have his cake and eat it too. That's why he was so conflicted. He could not reconcile his authentic/inauthentic personality and chose to take his own life because he could no longer suffer what he had become, blaming his electroshock treatment at the Mayo Clinic for destroying his memory. Which isn't to say there wasn't some truth to what he believed about ECT, but Hemingway had a long history of always blaming someone else for his own misery, and his personality was shadow-afflicted long before he received two treatments of ECT for his paranoia and depression.

So what did Rumi and Emily Dickinson know about the individuation of our essential nature that other writers can't seem to fathom but catch a glimpse of with every *"founding moment"* that they are blessed to witness or experience and write about?

I cannot count the number of times that I exclaimed in ecstatic excitement while talking with Penny about something or other, *"That's a poem!"* Or, *"That's a spiritual musing!"* Or, *"There's a story in that!"* Because in that moment of euphoric insight I caught a glimpse of the "meaning" behind what we were talking about, and that "meaning" was what Miriam Toews meant by a *"founding moment".* And by "meaning," I mean the essential truth of an experience, or what the poet Adrianne Rich called "a deeper perception of what is."

This is what all the excitement was about when Thomas Wolfe's alter ego shouted, "The *way*! The *way*? Do you understand?" He too caught a glimpse of the secret way of life which he called "the *way*," just as Hemingway caught a glimpse and called it "the secret that is poetry written into prose," and by poetry he meant what Rumi and Emily Dickinson had discovered and other poets pointed to with the genius of their own individual *way*.

A *"founding moment"* then is an event, be it an actual experience or epiphany, that parts the veils of life and gives one a glimpse at the bigger picture of man's existence, and this bigger picture is what the "spooky art" tries to discover, like I did when serendipity introduced me to a married ex-nun who was in fear of losing her Roman Catholic faith.

While painting the house that she and her husband had purchased when they moved from the east coast to my hometown in northern Ontario, the idea "came" to me to write a novel on her spiritual dilemma; and I wrote *Tea with Grace, A Story of Synchronicity and Platonic Love,* an intensely autobiographical novel that explored what happened to Grace when she came to a crossroads in her life, which makes a *"founding moment"* an entry point into the mystery of the "meaning" of life, thus confirming Alice Munro's aesthetic that fiction and not memoir is the truth of life, something that Hemingway knew instinctively and quite possibly another reason why I was called back to him...

38. Hemingway's Dilemma

Monday, May 15, 2017

I wrote a book called *Why Bother? The Riddle of the Good Samaritan* because I wanted to creatively explore Christ's parable of the good Samaritan, the fundamental premise of my book being the individuation process, and I wrote *The Lion that Swallowed Hemingway* because in Hemingway I saw that his *way* had taken him to a dead end; but not C. G. Jung, who also played a big part in my literary memoir because Jung's *way* took him all the way to wholeness and singleness of self, but why did Jung succeed and Hemingway fail?

"As each plant grows from a seed and becomes in the end an oak tree, so man must become what he is meant to be. He ought to get there, but most get stuck," said Jung, and he succeeded to become what he was meant to be because he was wise enough to reconcile himself with himself, which Hemingway could not do despite the integrative process of his writing which he devoted himself to with monastic discipline …

This morning I began to read Jung's *Red Book* again (I got it from Penny for a Christmas gift on *December 28, 2012* and finished reading it *January 1, 2013*, five days of the most satisfying reading in my life), and even though I had highlighted the sentence, it spoke to me loud and clear again this morning: **"There is only one way and that is your way."** (And in the footnotes the *Draft* continues: "only one law exists, and that is your law. Only one truth exists, and that is your truth.") This is why I fell in love with Jung, because he confirmed my own experience that **the way is and always will be an individual path**.

"This life is the way, the long sought-after way to the unfathomable, which we call divine. There is no other way, all other ways are false paths," wrote Jung in *The Red Book*; but one's *way* can take one to a dead end, as it did me many times; but *the omniscient guiding principle of life* always gave me a way out. This is the premise of my book *The Merciful Law of Divine Synchronicity.* Hemingway however got swallowed up by his own shadow and could not find a way out of his dilemma, and despair drove him to suicide.

Had not my call to writing in high school (actually, my call came in grade school, around the middle of grade seven or eight which was ignited by Hemingway in high school) been supplanted by my call to become a seeker like Maugham's hero Larry Darrell, I would never have discerned the secret way of literature; and because I succeeded in my quest and found my true self, I had enough gnostic wisdom to discern that life itself is the *way*, just as C. G. Jung experienced in his own remarkable journey of self-discovery.

This is why Hemingway's life spoke to me. I could "see" that he got stuck in his journey to what he was meant to be, and he got stuck because he became a prisoner of his own shadow-afflicted personality. His writing was his *way* out of himself, but because he could no longer write after two treatments of ECT at the Mayo Clinic he felt he had no reason left to live.

But as tragic as his suicide was, I have to admire and respect him for being true to himself. And I believe this is another reason I was called back to Hemingway, to illustrate with the great writer's life how one can get so stuck in their own personality that it can drive them to despair and even suicide. So, how exactly did my high school hero and literary mentor get so stuck in his ego/shadow personality that he could not save himself from himself?

I watched a YouTube video last night on a talk on Jung's *Red Book* given at the Library of Congress in Washington DC, which I had seen before two or three times already, and Ann Ulanov, a Jungian analyst and Professor of Psychiatry and Religion, quoted something that Jung wrote in *The Red Book* that speaks to the essential principle of the individual way. "Our task," said Jung, "is to live oneself, to fulfill what comes to you, for our life is the truth we seek. We create the truth by living it." "...*you make the path as you walk,"* said Paula Fox.

"In order to write about life first you must live it," said Hemingway, and live it he did; and from his vast and varied experience of life he found his own truth that he poured into stories that garnered him the Nobel Prize for Literature, "for his powerful,

style-forming mastery of the art of modern narration, as most recently evinced in 'The Old Man and the Sea'" said the Nobel Prize committee; but Hemingway's truth, like the truth of all literature, wasn't enough to set him free from the prison of his own ego/shadow personality, which begs the question: *how much truth does one need to become what one is meant to be?*

Is there a tipping point to one's truth? Can one's way garner enough truth to set one free from himself? This was the fundamental theme of my book *Why Bother? The Riddle of the Good Samaritan.* Using Christ's parable, I wanted to show that the way to gain "eternal life" and become what one is meant to be was to become a giver instead of a taker, which the rich young man in Christ's parable wasn't willing to do, and neither was Hemingway.

Hemingway was a taker all his life. His mother saw his selfish nature and admonished him in a stern, ominously prophetic letter that she wrote to him when he loafed around doing nothing for months on end after he came home from Italy a wounded war hero. "Unless you, my son Ernest, come to yourself," she wrote; "cease your lazy loafing and pleasure seeking; borrowing with no thought of returning; stop trying to graft a living off anybody and everybody; spending all your earnings lavishly and wastefully on luxuries for yourself; stop trading on your handsome face to fool little gullible girls, and neglecting your duties to God and your Savior Jesus Christ; unless, in other words, you come into your manhood, there is nothing for you but bankruptcy…" (*Ernest Hemingway: A Life Story*, Carols Baker, p.97).

Ernest Hemingway took and took and took because he lived for his writing and all the pleasure he could get out of life, and he grew in his own truth of always taking to satisfy his feverish longing to become the greatest writer of his generation; but his truth could not set him free from himself because his truth, as profoundly existential as it was, did not hold the key to the prison door of his ego/shadow personality, which was why Sartre found in Hemingway a writer who reflected his no-exit philosophy of life.

Jung, on the other hand, found the key to his prison in the truth of his "confrontation with the unconscious" which changed the dynamic of his ego-shadow personality. "In the fortieth year of my life, I had achieved everything that I had wished for myself. I had achieved honor, power, wealth, knowledge, and every human happiness. Then my desire for the increase of these trappings ceased, the desire ebbed from me and horror came over me...My soul, where are you? Do you hear me? I call you—are you there? I have returned. I am here again..." wrote Jung in *The Red Book,* thus beginning his quest for his soul which he lost in his ego/shadow personality; and in his journey into the depths of the unconscious he learned that to save himself from himself he had to stop taking from life and become a giver, and he devoted the rest of his life to exploring the secret way and transmitting the sacred knowledge of integrating the inner and outer self of man through his psychology of individuation.

Victor Frankl came to the same realization in the concentration camps: "A thought transfixed me: for the first time in my life I saw the truth as it is set into song by so many poets, proclaimed as the final wisdom by so many thinkers. The truth—that love is the ultimate and highest goal to which man can aspire. Then I grasped the meaning of the greatest secret that human poetry and human thought and belief have to impart: *The salvation of man is through love and in love"* (*Man's Search for Meaning,* Victor Frankl, p. 57).

This was the underlying motif of my book *The Lion that Swallowed Hemingway,* to which this journal on my writing life will be a sequel, because Hemingway and Jung represent the two sides of the *enantiodromiac* dynamic of our ego/shadow personality. Both of my heroes dared to live their own life; but Hemingway's *way* took him so deep into his ego/shadow personality that he lost himself, and Jung's *way* transformed his ego/shadow personality and set him free from himself. Two exceptional men, two *ways* of life, but separate truths; and that's the mystery of the secret way of life that literature struggles to realize...

39. Why Do Writer's Write?

Wednesday, May 17, 2017

I had no desire to read Hemingway yesterday (I'm well into my second reading of *The Hemingway Women*, by Bernice Kert and almost finished another reading of *Winner Take Nothing*, Hemingway's early book of short stories), and instead I picked up *Writers On Writing, Volume II, More Collected Essays from The New Yorker,* that was sitting on my stairwell with a dozen other books, and I sat on the front deck and read it through because the private life and thoughts and creative process of other writers fascinates me.

Writers are very much like other people. We look the same as other people, and may even talk the same, though not really, and we have similar wants and needs, but for all of our sameness writers are different from other people simple because we are writers.

Writers are called to writing, and because of our calling we are different. Not everyone is called to their path, or individual way of life if you will; but when a person is called to their path by life—be it music, art, medicine, politics or whatever—one is automatically different from everyone that has not yet been called because they aren't ready to begin the long process of self-reconciliation that life expects of those it calls; that's what makes us different.

In his own way, Victor Frankl realized this in the Nazi concentration camps (his father, mother, brother, and his wife died in the camps or were sent to gas ovens), the astonishing realization that *life was not created for man's purpose, but man for life's purpose;* and a calling to one's path is a calling to life's purpose which, sadly, very few people realize.

"Many are called, but few are chosen," said Jesus, and few are chosen because they have not evolved enough in their own identity yet to "see" and "hear" what Thomas Wolfe and Ernest Hemingway and many writers have caught a glimpse of—the *"way,"* the secret path to wholeness and singleness of self that we are all called to eventually.

Margaret Atwood, a well-known Canadian writer was called to writing. In her essay "A Path Taken with All the Certainty of Youth," she writes: "How is it that I became a writer? It wasn't a likely thing for me to have done, nor was it something that I chose, as you might choose to be a lawyer or a dentist. It simply happened, suddenly, in 1956, while I was crossing the football field on the way home from school. I wrote a poem in my head and then I wrote it down, and after that, writing was the only thing I wanted to do" (*Writers on Writing, Volume II,* p. 9); a calling to the writer's way, if ever there was one.

But I cannot read Margaret Atwood. Believe me, I tried; but I simply cannot read her writing. Not that she isn't a brilliant writer. She's acquired mastery over many genres, beginning with poetry and moving on to short stories, novels, essays, plays and whatnot (she keeps expanding her paradigm), but her perspective on life frightens me no less than the stare of Medusa's eyes, which for some strange reason she looks like to me with her electrified hair and stare, and even talks as I would imagine Medusa would talk, her voice instantly sending me into a deep freeze, and all because her truth does not resonate with me. So dissonant is it in fact that whenever I hear her talking on the radio or TV, I have to turn her off.

But why? What is it about her personal truth that affects me this way? And why does she have such a large readership when she gives me the creeps? As a matter of fact, as I write this journal entry a dramatic series based on her dystopian novel *A Handmaid's Tale* is playing on TV (a Hollywood movie was already made on her disquieting novel, which I refused to see); so what is it about her personal truth that bothers me?

If my memory serves me, one line of her poetry that I read many years ago speaks to my dissonance with Margaret Atwood's dystopian view of the world: "All we have is hope, but what hope is there?" I, on the other hand, don't see life this way.

What does she mean by her question "what hope is there?" if not to imply that there is no way out of the Sisyphean struggle of life? Like Camus, she embraces the meaninglessness and absurdity of life and valiantly tries to make the best of it, and she is valiant in her efforts to save the environment and help the underdog whenever she can; but as free as she is to choose how to live her life within the paradigm of her personal truth, Atwood's freedom condemns her to the nothingness of man's existence, which is only one half of the "tale told by an idiot full of sound and fury" that she takes to be the whole story...

40. Hemingway's Miserable Soul

Thursday, May 18, 2017

One cannot become what he is meant to be in one lifetime alone. That's the catch that stumps most people who seek to know the meaning and purpose of life, and not until one embraces the concept of reincarnation and live within the paradigm of karmic choices and consequences will one begin to see that the path they are called to was forged in the soul of their many lives, and the path they are called to begins the long process of what Socrates called "the habit of soul gathering and collecting herself into herself," as I was called to in my past lifetime when I was a student of Pythagoras who taught us the sacred teachings of the secret way of self-reconciliation and called to again in my current lifetime with Gurdjieff's teaching of "work on oneself" which opened me up again to the secret way of life.

I love Gurdjieff's parable of the two chairs. *"Happy is the man who has a chair to sit on, unhappy is the man who has no chair to sit on, but woe to the man who stands between two chairs,"* which he later translated for his pupils into the saying that was inscribed into a special script of his powerful sayings that hung above the walls of the Study House at the Institute for the Harmonious Development of Man in Fontainebleau, France: *"Blessed is he who has a soul, blessed is he who has none, but woe and grief to him who has it in embryo."*

Gurdjieff did not believe that man is born with an immortal soul. Under very special circumstances, one could create their own soul, and this soul, according to Gurdjieff would reincarnate; otherwise man would die and become *"merde."*

"Merde" is the French word for shit, fertilizer for Mother Nature; that's how Gurdjieff crudely put it. But man could create his own soul if he knew how. Gurdjieff travelled the East and Far East to find the secret teachings of the *way*, the mystical art of "creating" one's own soul; and when he found the *way* he introduced it to the western world as a system of "work on oneself" that transformed one's consciousness and immortalized one's essential nature.

That's the gist of Gurdjieff's teaching. But he was wrong about man's soul. I didn't know that he was wrong when I discovered Gurdjieff in Ouspensky's book *In Search of the Miraculous*, but I *knew* that his teaching was the path I had to take to find my true self; and I "worked" on myself until I realized my immortal nature in my mother's kitchen that summer day while she kneaded bread dough on the kitchen table. And years later when Penny and I moved to Georgian Bay I had seven past-life regressions and learned that we are all born with a spark of divine consciousness, and through the merciful law of reincarnation we grow into our own identity until we realize our divine nature; so as wrong as he was about man not being born with an immortal soul, Gurdjieff's teaching sped up the process of self-realization, and this was the premise of my book *Gurdjieff Was Wrong But His Teaching Works.*

That's why I have an natural dissonance with Margaret Atwood and all writers who limit man's existence to one lifetime alone, especially when they are so crystallized in their belief system like the "Medusa" of literature; but that's what happens to one who has no chair to sit on: they are obtusely content in their spiritual ignorance.

But not the person who stands between two chairs. He's in the throes of "creating" his own soul, and his life is miserable—like Hemingway. This is why I was called to Hemingway in high school. I was torn between two chairs also, and I had to learn from his life experience, which I did and wrote about in my literary memoir *The Lion that Swallowed Hemingway*; but apparently I had still more to learn, and serendipity brought me back to my high school hero and literary mentor with the *Hemingway Notebook* that I got for Christmas from Penny's sister. But what does it mean to stand between two chairs?

It's taken years of dialectical writing (by this I mean engaging what Jung called my "transcendent function") to work out this complex aspect of man's *enantiodromiac* nature—the constant give-and-take of man's *being* and *non-being*, what Gurdjieff called *essence* and *personality* and what I simply call man's real and false self; and a man who stands between two chairs is torn between his real and false self and is miserable in his life.

Miserable people aren't bad people, as such; that's what I came to realize after years of studying the *enantiodromiac dynamic* of the natural process of individuation, the never-ending conflict in one's soul that Hemingway exemplified in panoramic color with his larger than life personality that he fostered to feed his insatiable ego and advance his career, but he suffered trying to keep his false self from swallowing him whole, which it finally did.

That's the dynamic of Hemingway's individuation process, and I was called back to him so I can bring some measure of compassionate understanding to his miserable soul, because despite his monstrously cruel and insensitive ego he wasn't a bad person. To repeat what his friend and poet Archibald MacLeish said to Denis Brian for his book *The True Gen*, "He was one of the most human and spiritually powerful creatures I have ever known."

"Human" because he was torn between his false and real self, like the vast majority of mankind, and "spiritually powerful" because he was called to his path of self-reconciliation through writing which tested him in ways that few people can appreciate. I know, because I was torn between my real and false self to the point where I *had* to choose, and out of my choice was born the meanest saying of my life: *"The shortest way to God is through hell."*

That's why I empathize with the great writer...

41. The Writer's Way

Friday, May 19, 2017

The writer's way is the way of literature, and the way of literature is the secret way of life, the gnostic wisdom of life's purpose and meaning wrought out of life experience. This is what makes literature so fascinating. It speaks to the universal truth of life's purpose and meaning through the writer's personal experience, the secret way of life lived individually.

I recently discovered two writers who speak to the secret way of life: Paula Fox, who gave me the strongest impression that she had a chair to sit on and had to carve out her own path to what she was meant to be *("I think you make the path as you walk,"* she said on CBC's *Writer's & Company),* which she chronicled in her novels; and Pat Conroy, whose troubled life shouted from the rooftops that he stood between two chairs like his literary hero Thomas Wolfe, Ernest Hemingway and myself, and who said, "I write to explain my own life to myself." But what was Pat Conroy trying to explain if not the mystery of his own *becoming*, the individuation process of his own identity like every other writer?

Despite his misperception that man is not born with an immortal soul, Gurdjieff's parable of the two chairs goes a long way to demystifying the natural individuation process of the inner and outer self of man, and had I not reconciled with myself and become what I was meant to be I would not be journaling about my writing life and the secret way; but because I found my true self, I saw that the secret way was the way of literature, just as young Pat Conroy intuited when he fell under the spell of Thomas Wolfe when his English teacher gave him a copy of Wolfe's first novel, *Look Homeward, Angel.*

"*Look Homeward, Angel* was the text of my liberation into myself, the one that gave me access to the ceremonies and procedures that would lead me to the writer's way," wrote Pat Conroy in his introduction to the anniversary edition of Thomas Wolfe's novel *Of*

Time and the River, which was Conroy's calling to become what he was meant to be through the integrative process of creative writing, a perfect illustration of the natural individuation process of the way of literature that Conroy explored in his own intensely autobiographical novels, like *The Great Santini, The Lords of Discipline,* and *The Prince of Tides* which were made into Hollywood movies that I saw and loved very much.

"To become a writer, I knew I had to stagger through my world with an insatiable lust for life, for the raw hunks of indigestible experience, for soaking up the million-footed images that would be thrown my way," wrote Conroy, and he did become a writer who gave light to the individuation process in his novels which chronicle his own *enantiodromiac dynamic* of standing between two chairs that was so devastatingly personal that his novels singed the soul of family members; but that's what Wolfe did with his first novel *Look Homeward, Angel* which so offended the people of his home town that he was reviled for years, just as I was by the people of my own hometown when I self-published my novel *What Would I Say Today If I Were To Die Tomorrow?* that showed them in a light they did not want to be seen...

The writer's way is not easy, but it IS the way of life; and that's the connection that Pat Conroy finally made as he tried to explain his life to himself in his novels. When his English teacher gave him an apple from the tree in the back-yard of the boarding house in Asheville, North Carolina where Thomas Wolfe had grown up and commanded him to eat it, Eugene Norris wanted the aspiring young writer to see that there *was* a relationship between life and art; and when Conroy became a successful writer and was asked by Paramount Pictures to write a screen play for the novel *Look Homeward, Angel* he placed a call from Los Angeles to his former teacher to share his good news and pay respect to him for his guidance.

"That's something, Pat. That's not nothing, boy. That's something," his old English teacher replied, glowing with pride for his former student. "Who else have you called?"

"No one yet, Gene. I wanted you to be the first," Pat said.

"Why me?" Gene asked.

"Because, Gene, great English teacher, I wanted to let you know you were right. There IS a relationship between life and art," replied the now-seasoned writer who suffered an immortal wound when his mentoring teacher introduced him to Thomas Wolfe.

Through Thomas Wolfe's writing and lust for life, Pat Conroy found his own writer's way which began the long and insufferable process of self-reconciliation that he chronicled in his own novels, like Hemingway chronicled his own conflicted life; and though I'm a little-known writer living in Tiny Beaches, Georgian Bay I also chronicled my own life in stories, novels, poetry, spiritual musings, and memoirs; but because I reconciled myself with myself, I have a larger perspective than the writer's way, and this is what I hope to convey in my new call back to my high school hero and literary mentor, Ernest "Papa" Hemingway...

42. Stuffed Birds and Personal Experience

Saturday, May 20, 2017

"Is belief anything more than a trope for you now?" *The Paris Review* interviewer Antonio Weiss asked Professor Harold Bloom in the Spring 1991 edition of the magazine, and Bloom replied: "Belief is not available to me. It is a stuffed bird, up on the shelf. So is philosophy, let me point out, and so, for that matter, is psychoanalysis—an institutional church founded upon Freud's writings, praxis, and example. These are not live birds that one can hold in one's hand. We live in a literary culture, as I keep saying. This is not necessarily good—it might even be bad—but it is where we are. Our cognitive modes have failed us."

I went online yesterday to read the Bloom interview "The Art of Criticism" in *The Paris Review* because I relish listening to Professor Bloom speaking off the cuff, his vast knowledge of literature and phenomenal memory never ceasing to amaze me (he never used notes to teach his students), and what he said about beliefs spoke directly to the way of literature, because the way of literature is not about beliefs but the truth and meaning of life experience; this is why Hemingway said that when he read Tolstoy's *War and Peace* he skipped all the philosophizing parts and went straight to the story because that was Tolstoy's personal experience, albeit heightened by the magnificent powers of his imagination.

"The needful thing is not to know the truth but to experience it. Not to have an intellectual conception of things, but to find our way to the inner, and perhaps wordless, irrational experience, "said C. G. Jung in Ann Belford Ulanov's book *Spirit in Jung;* this is why I wrote a spiritual musing called "Do We Choose Our Beliefs or Do They Choose Us?" which can be found in my book *The Merciful Law of Divine Synchronicity*: I wanted to make the distinction between "stuffed birds" and personal experience…

I'm reading *The Complete Short Stories of Ernest Hemingway* and his posthumous novels *True at First Light* and *The Garden of Eden* and almost finished Baker's *Ernest Hemingway: A Life Story,* and I can't get over how much Hemingway drew upon his personal experiences for his short stories and novels, which of course were aesthetically enhanced by his existentially grounded imagination, and given what I knew about Wolfe and other writers and what I recently discovered about Pat Conroy and Paula Fox, two remarkable writers who also drew directly upon their own experiences for their novels, I'm beyond conviction in my intuition that the writer's way is the way of literature, the *enantiodromiac dynamic* of the individuation process of man's ego/shadow personality; which is why Professor Bloom said that we live in a literary culture because the "cognitive modes have failed us."

This speaks to the ontology of our *being* and *non-being*, the dual consciousness of our individuating essential self (I hesitate to call it our soul self, but that's what our essential self is as I experienced in my past-life regressions), and when our beliefs keep our essential self prisoner to our personality we become trapped in the non-reality of our *being*—or, if you will, in the reality of our *non-being,* for such is the paradoxical nature of our real and false self. This is why for all of his genius the "god of literature" could not find a way out of man's prison, which led Professor Bloom to call Shakespeare's world "a breathtaking kind of nihilism."

"Man must complete what nature cannot finish," said the ancient alchemists, which Gurdjieff repeated when he told his students that nature will only evolve man so far and then he/she must take evolution into their own hands; but this only makes sense within the paradigm of reincarnation, because it is simply impossible for man to realize his essential nature in the span of one lifetime alone; this is why literature cannot satisfy the longing in one's soul for wholeness and completeness, as the New Zealand writer Katherine Mansfield realized. To complete what Nature cannot finish, man must transcend himself; and this is what the way of literature points to, if one has the courage to see it. But how?

How can man complete what nature cannot finish? How can man escape from the prison of their own ego/shadow personality and realize their essential nature? This was the theme of my spiritual musing "The Prison of Personality" that I included in my memoir *The Merciful Law of Divine Synchronicity*, because I wanted to show that there is a way out of the dilemma of our paradoxical nature, and that way out is the secret way of life that literature points to, as Emily Dickinson intuits in her riddling verse: "Adventure most unto itself /The Soul condemned to be; /Attended by a Single Hound—/Its own Identity."

Again, this is why I was called back to Hemingway, to reaffirm what I wrote in *The Lion that Swallowed Hemingway*, but with more cognitive awareness this time; because since I wrote *The Lion that Swallowed Hemingway* three years ago, I've grown in my understanding of the limits of literature and feel much more sympathy for writers like Hemingway who trap themselves in their ego/shadow personality and cannot escape themselves...

In his *Paris Review* interview, Professor Bloom was asked how he managed to write so quickly, if it was insomnia (he was sixty at the time and continued to pour out books well into his eighties), and, strangely enough, Bloom attributed his prodigious output to the limitations of the way of literature that he had devoted his whole life to.

"Partly insomnia," he replied, with melancholy. "I think I usually write therapeutically. That is what Hart Crane really taught one. (Bloom read all of Crane before he was twelve and continued to read him all his life.) I was talking to William Empson about this once. He never wrote any criticism of Crane, and he didn't know whether he liked his poetry or not, but he said that the desperation of Crane's poetry appealed to him. Using his funny kind of parlance, he said that Hart Crane's poetry showed that poetry is now a mug's game, that Crane always wrote every poem as though it were going to be his last. That catches something in Crane which is very true, that he writes each lyric in such a way that you literally feel he's going to die if he can't bring it off, that his survival not just as a poet but as a person depends upon somehow articulating that poem. I don't have the audacity to compare myself to Crane, yet I think I write criticism in the spirit in which he wrote poems. One writes to keep going, to keep oneself from going mad. One writes to be able to write the next piece of criticism or to live through the next day or two. Maybe it's an apotropaic gesture, maybe one writes to ward off death. I'm not sure. But I think in some sense that's what poets do. They write their poems to ward off dying."

How ironic. Professor Bloom as much as tells us that literature is not enough to satisfy the longing in one's soul for wholeness, and the fear of death keeps him writing, as I'm sure it does most writers, especially Hemingway who pushed this fear to the extreme when he confessed to his young friend Aaron Hotchner in *Papa Hemingway* that he didn't want to live if he could no longer write; this is why Professor Bloom explored the wisdom literature of the world, to look for a way out of the nihilism, however breathtaking, of literature.

But even after writing such magnificent books as *Genius: One Hundred Exemplary Creative Minds, Shakespeare: The Invention of the Human, The Shadow of a Great Rock: A Literary Appreciation of the King James Bible,* and other books that explore the genius and wisdom of literature like *Novelists and Novels, The Western Canon,* and *The Daimon Knows,* Professor Bloom could not find the hidden key that opened the door to the way out of literature. "…and none shall make discovery," said Emily Dickinson:

This Consciousness that is aware
Of Neighbors and the Sun
Will be the one aware of Death
And that itself alone

Is traversing the interval
Experience between
And most profound experiment
Appointed unto Men –

How adequate unto itself
Its properties shall be
Itself unto itself and none
Shall make discovery.

Adventure most unto itself
The soul condemned to be –
Attended by a single Hound

Its own identity.

Professor Bloom came to the same conclusion in *The Western Canon* when he wrote "primarily each ambitious writer is out for himself alone and will frequently betray or neglect his class in order to advance his own interests, which center entirely upon *individuation*," but if literature and "stuffed birds" are not enough to satisfy man's longing for wholeness, where does one turn? That's the central issue of my call back to Hemingway...

43. The Flaw in Hemingway's Logic

Monday, May 22, 2017

Something I read in Carlos Baker's biography this morning alerted me to the flaw in Hemingway's logic, something I felt for many years but could not bring myself to acknowledge because I did not have enough literary knowledge or writing experience to believe it; but I must have now or this shattering insight would not have surfaced, and basically it has to do with Hemingway's character; or more specifically, his literary integrity.

Before I went to university I was a salesman for a product called USC (University Scholarships of Canada), a scholarship fund that we sold to parents for their newborn child's higher education, and I was trained by an experienced salesman to hit the buyer between the eyes with the bottom line first, and then take them down slowly, which I feel I should do with the flaw in Hemingway's logic; so, here's my bottom line: *Hemingway cheated.*

I don't mean that he cheated on his four wives, he certainly did that; and I don't mean that he cheated with the truth when talking about himself, he certainly did that too (which is why his independently minded third wife called him a pathological liar and apocryphiar); I mean that he cheated in his writing, which is very difficult to believe because Hemingway based the whole aesthetic of his writing upon the *one true sentence principle* and *telling it the way it was.* So what do I mean when I say that Hemingway cheated in his writing?

Baker tells us that Hemingway submitted four new stories to *Scribner's Magazine* one year which were to be published in the spring. The stories were "A Clean, Well-Lighted Place," "Homage to Switzerland," "The Gambler, the Nun, and the Radio," and "The Light of the World." The new editor at *Scribner's* Alfred Dashiel accepted the first three for publication but rejected the fourth because "Dashiel believed, not without reason, that it was far too outspoken for the clientele his magazine served. Little did Dashiel know, said

Ernest, how much concealed dynamite lay in the stories already accepted," wrote Baker.

I read these stories several times, my favorite being "A Clean, Well-Lighted Place" because it spoke to Hemingway's fear of nothingness (the pervasive feeling that one gets when one's dark side casts its "shadow" upon one's ego personality), but when the new *Scribner's* editor Alfred Dashiel rejected "The Light of the World," "an ultra-tough story about a group of whores at a railroad station in a small town in northern Michigan," the slighted Hemingway's response was that he didn't really much care because the other stories had enough "concealed dynamite" in them to make up for the story the new editor at *Scribner's Magazine* Alfred Dashiel, "whom Ernest never tired of criticizing," rejected, which in Hemingway's mind gave him the last word. That was Hemingway, right or wrong he had to have the last word; but what did he mean by "concealed dynamite"?

Obviously, it was a reference to his "iceberg theory," that part of his story that was hidden within the body of the story like seven eighths of the iceberg is hidden from sight; and that's when my uneasy feeling about Hemingway's personal aesthetic surfaced and made itself conscious as the flaw in the great writer's logic.

In short, it finally dawned on me that the "concealed dynamite" of his stories was nothing more than a clever literary device to make his stories intriguing and alluring, like Jake Barnes's sexual problem in *The Sun Also Rises*, a problem that haunts the whole novel and keeps the reader wondering why he and Lady Brett Ashley never got it on, as the saying goes; but why would I feel that Hemingway was cheating?

Did he not trust the truth of his stories? Did he have to trick the reader by hiding the truth in the body of his stories, and by truth I mean the gnostic wisdom of the secret way of life that Hemingway extracted from his life experience that inspired his stories, the truth of the *enantiodromiac* dynamic of man's becoming, like his creative insight into the horrifying nothingness of life in "A Clean, Well-Lighted Place"? Why did I feel that he cheated by hiding the truth of life in the body of his stories and novels?

I could never put my finger on it, but deep inside I *knew* there was something devious about Hemingway's "iceberg theory," the clever way it manipulated the reader's sensibilities, and had not this morning's spontaneous insight reminded me of a poem I wrote for my book of poetry *Not My Circus, Not My Monkeys*, I would never have caught Hemingway's clever literary devil by the tail: —

Pinning the Devil Down

I hate it when a poet
tries to be profound with
what he does not know, forever
struggling to free himself from
his shallow grave;

and I hate it when a poet
tries to be cavalier with deadly
serious matters, making out
like he's above the fray;

and I hate it when a poet
assumes an air he has not earned,
wearing the poet's mantle
for authority;

but I hate it most when a poet
gets it right, because he's pinned
the devil down and wrestled all the wit,
charm, and deceit out of him!

During his formative years in Paris, the charming young Hemingway used writers like Scott Fitzgerald (who advised Hemingway to delete the long superfluous beginning of *The Sun Also Rises* because it did not set the right tone for the novel, which Hemingway did but who never credited Fitzgerald for that editorial piece of advice that helped make his novel a popular and brilliant literary success), Gertrude Stein, Ezra Pound, Ford Maddox Ford, James Joyce, and journalists and magazine editors, sucking everything he could get out of them that would help improve the quality of his stories to make them marketable, all the while reading copiously and assiduously studying the best writers he could get his hands on from Sylvia Beach's bookstore and lending library *Shakespeare and Company*, like Chekov, Turgenev, Maupassant, Dostoevsky and Joseph Conrad that helped him cultivate a style of his own which he honed with lapidary precision when he discovered "cablese" while practicing journalism; but apart from his spartan prose that made his stories eminently readable, it was the literary device of his "iceberg theory" that gave his stories a certain mystique that launched Hemingway into the literary stratosphere, and not without deserved credit; but still, I feel he cheated, which could be why in his most autobiographical short story "The Snows of Kilimanjaro," about a dying writer taking stock of his wasted life, Hemingway included by way of introduction to his story a local legend about a dried and frozen carcass of a leopard found near the western summit of Mount Kilimanjaro, which the Masai called "the House of God." "No one had explained what the leopard was seeking at that altitude," said the legend; but I'd bet my bottom dollar that Hemingway knew…

44. Hemingway's Double

Tuesday, May 23, 2017

We all have a double. Our double is identical to us in every way but one. It looks like us, it talks like us, it does everything we do like us, but it is not who we are; it is the opposite of who we are. Our double is our false self. It is our shadow.

"The shadow goes by many familiar names: the disowned self, the lower self, the dark twin or brother, the double, repressed self, alter ego, id. When we come face to face with our darker side, we use metaphors to describe these shadow encounters: meeting our demons, wrestling with the devil, decent into the underworld, dark night of the soul, midlife crisis," wrote the editors Connie Zweig and Jeremiah Abrams in their introduction to *Meeting the Shadow: The Hidden Dark Side of Human Nature*, further articulating that "the ego stands to the shadow as light to shade."

It was their gifted, intuitive awareness of the dark shadow side of the ego personality that led Theodor Dostoevsky to write his novel *The Double*, Oscar Wilde to write *The Picture of Dorian Gray*, and Robert Louis Stevenson *The Strange Case of Dr. Jekyll and Mr. Hyde,* all stories about the dark side of human nature; but how does the shadow side of our ego personality develop? Where does it come from?

"The personal shadow develops naturally in every young child," wrote the editors of *Meeting the Shadow*. "As we identify with ideal personality characteristics such as politeness and generosity, which are reinforced in our environment, we shape what W. Brugh Joy calls the New Year's Resolution Self," which simple means our best self, or acceptable public persona; however, "at the same time we bury in the shadow those qualities that don't fit our self-image, such as rudeness and selfishness. The ego and the shadow, then, develop in tandem, creating each out of the same life experience," say Zweig and Abrams.

Not only do we have a personal shadow, we have a family shadow as well; and our family shadow becomes part of our personal shadow. We inherit our family shadow just as we inherit biological traits from our parents and ancestors. This is the psychological explanation for the old saying "the sins of the parents are visited upon the children."

"For different people, in different families and cultures, what falls into ego and what falls into shadow can vary," say Zweig and Abrams. Nonetheless, "all the feelings and capacities that are rejected by the ego and exiled into the shadow contribute to the hidden power of the dark side of human nature." Because the shadow is the unconscious underside of our ego personality it is by its very nature difficult to apprehend, and it is "dangerous, disorderly, and forever in hiding, as if the light of consciousness would steal its very life."

This is the mystery of our shadow double. It does not want to be seen, because being seen it is in danger of being dealt with consciously; but such is the dynamic of the natural individuation process of our evolving essential self, the shadow can overwhelm and possess the ego personality without one being aware of it, which prompted Carl Jung to say, in serious jest, "How do you find a lion that has swallowed you?"

This is why I gave a copy of my book *The Lion that Swallowed Hemingway* to a neighbor who moved into the house across from us, a man whom I perceived to be so shadow-afflicted that I thought it would do him good to catch a glimpse of his dark side by reading my story of how Hemingway got swallowed up by his own dark shadow; but to no avail.

But then, Jung did say that it takes great moral courage to see our own shadow; this is why few people want to become aware of their dark side, because it would demand of one to take moral responsibility for their double. This was the conflict that Robert Louis Stevenson explored in his psychological novel: Dr. Jekyll was responsible for Mr. Hyde.

And so was Dorian Gray responsible for the soul-portrait of his dark double hidden away from sight in the attic of his house and which became darker and darker with every new sin that Dorian Gray committed, for such is how our double grows.

Our double grows according to the values we live by, and if our values are less than what our family and society deem acceptable our double grows and grows and grows until it has an autonomy of its own; and that's what happened to Hemingway...

Because I believe in reincarnation, my understanding of the shadow self includes our past-life personalities, which I confirmed with my own seven past-life regressions; this gave my insight into our double all the latitude I needed to make sense of my own shadow-afflicted personality, and the reason I had to absolve myself of myself. That's why I went on my quest for my real self which I've written about in *The Pearl of Great Price, The Summoning of Noman*, and *Gurdjieff Was Wrong But His Teaching Works*; and the reason I wrote *The Lion that Swallowed Hemingway*, because I knew the geography of my soul very well.

During the summer months while I was going to university, I worked waiting on tables at the Nipigon Inn Hotel after my day job, and I made an observation about people during the course of the evening that I could not explain until I grew in my understanding of the shadow side of our ego personality. The observation I made was the change in personality my customers underwent, without their being aware of it, the more inebriated they became; and this change in their personality intrigued me for a long time until I came to the see that alcohol has a way of bringing one's shadow out of hiding. But why?

The answer I came to was that the more inebriated one gets, the more one's personality relaxes its hold upon its shadow, and when one gets really drunk the shadow has free play, just like in the short story "Counterparts" that I read the other day in Joyce's *Dubliners.*

It was no coincidence that Joyce called his story "Counterparts," because he wanted his title to convey his main character's shadow-afflicted personality, a man called Farrington who thinks more of himself than is good for him. He's thin skinned and slights easily, which his supervisor on his job does in the story; and, of course, he's a drinker. And with brilliant story-telling expertise, Joyce reveals the slow emergence of Farrington's shadow double (counterpart) the more inebriated Farrington gets in the pubs that he went to after work the day he got slighted by his supervisor, ending up at home drunk and abusive to his family because drinking brought out the dark, nasty side of his personality.

The definition of "counterpart" is "a thing that fits another perfectly," "one remarkably similar to another," which describes the shadow double perfectly, and Joyce, well known for his own drinking and intimate familiarity with Irish pubs, drew a perfect picture of how the shadow double has a way of coming out the more drunk one gets, as Farrington's counterpart does in Joyce's story; and this describes the alcoholic Ernest "Papa" Hemingway, because the drunker Hemingway got the nastier he became.

Leonard Butts of the University of Cincinnati in *Studies in the Novel* thought that Jeffery Meyers, who wrote a four volume biography on Hemingway's life, portrayed him as "a cruel, selfish, sadistic, masochistic, and overbearing braggart who got what he deserved when friends and relatives rejected him and critics skewered him and his works," and Jeffery Meyers replied to Leonard Butts: "I'm not trying to put down Hemingway. I'm trying to tell the full story of his life" (*The True Gen*, by Denis Brian, p. 283).

"He's the cruelest man I know, and I have known some cruel men," said the wife who got away on him, and anyone who knew Hemingway personally experienced his mean-spirited, nasty double; especially his fourth wife Mary who suffered the brutality of his dark side through his nastiest moods, deepest depressions, paranoia, and suicide.

"Hemingway paid for his fun," wrote Brian in *The True Gen.* "He complained in letters to a friend in Spain that he was subjected by Mary to a nightly barrage of complaints that he was a heartless, selfish, stupid, spoiled, egotistical son-of-bitch." That's why I wrote *The Lion that Swallowed Hemingway*, to show the distinction between a man who got swallowed up by his own shadow and a man who had the moral courage to overcome his shadow and assimilate it into his ego personality, as Carl Gustav Jung did; and, of course, I wrote my story drawing upon my own experience of self-reconciliation which gave me the perspective to understand both the negative and positive sides of the individuation process...

45. Hemingway Cheated the Devil

Wednesday, May 24, 2017

By "working" on myself with Gurdjieff's teaching, I transformed my shadow-afflicted personality to the point where my own mother said to me one day, "You change before my eyes," and the mother of a friend I went to high school with said to me, "You're different. I don't know what it is about you, but you're different. You're not the same person."

What was different about me was that my shadow-afflicted personality was being transformed into a new personality, one that absorbed the dark shadow side of my nature and made it lighter; and I did this by "working" on myself with Gurdjieff's teaching and consciously practicing a life of virtue, which led me to see that there is an inherently self-transcending value to living a life guided by the noble virtues.

That's how I came to understand that *we can overcome the dark side of our nature by changing the values we live by*, which Hemingway refused to do because he made it his first priority to get all the pleasure that he could out of life, as his official biographer tells us when Hemingway compared his life to his alcoholic friend Scott Fitzgerald whose "cheap Irish love of defeat" was becoming tiresome to him: "Ernest, on the other hand, said that he had a damn good time all the time. When he was able to work, he never felt low. He took great pleasure in living 340 days out of every 365. He was always conscious, he said, of living not one life but two. One was that of a writer who got his reward after his death, and to hell with what he got now. The other was that of a man who got his everything now, and to hell with what came to him after death" (*Ernest Hemingway: A Life Story*, by Carlos Baker, p. 305).

A double life, to be sure; but as Denis Brian tells us in *The True Gen*, "Hemingway paid for his fun," and in more ways than one; but what really fascinated me about my high school hero and literary mentor was how he learned to cheat the devil by stealing precious élan from people, especially from his wives and other women, the younger the better, like the aristocratic young Venetian Adriana Ivancich who became the model for his beautiful Renata in *Across the River and into the Trees* that showed Hemingway at his most pathetic, shadow-afflicted deluded self in the aging Colonel Cantwell who was besotted by Renata as Hemingway was with Adrianna; but what does it mean to cheat the devil?

"I said last time," said G. I. Gurdjieff in Ouspensky's book *In Search of the Miraculous*, "that immortality is not a property with which man is born. But man can acquire immortality. All existing and generally known ways to immortality can be divided into three categories: 1. *The way of the fakir*, 2. *The way of the monk*, 3. *The way of the yogi*," and then Gurdjieff went on to say that there was another way, which he called the fourth way.

"The fourth way is sometimes called *the way of the sly man*. The 'sly man' knows some secret which the fakir, monk, and yogi do not know. How the 'sly man' learned this secret—it is not known. Perhaps he found it in some old book, perhaps he inherited it, perhaps he bought it, perhaps he stole it from someone. It makes no difference. The 'sly man' knows the secret and with its help outstrip the fakir, the monk, and the yogi" (*In Search of the Miraculous*, by P. D. Ouspensky, pp. 44, 50).

I acquired the secret of the sly man, not by reading about it, finding it in some old book, stealing it, nor did I purchase it; I acquired it slowly as I "worked" on myself with Gurdjieff's teaching of *conscious effort* and *intentional suffering, non-identifying* with the objects of my desire, and *self-remembering,* and by the severe discipline of living by higher values, the highest value being the virtue of Goodness; but had it not been for my *Royal Dictum* (my edict of self-denial), I would never have acquired the secret of the sly man, because the more I denied myself the pleasures of life the more I kept my own shadow from stealing my precious élan that I created daily by "working" my trade to the best of my ability and with honesty and integrity, élan which I called "virtue" that I desperately needed to "create" my own soul and which I began to see could easily be stolen from me if I did not guard myself against my own dark shadow double and the devious devil cheaters of the world.

"If thou hast not seen the devil, look at thine own self," said Rumi; and by devil he meant our own dark shadow double. And a devil cheater is someone who steals élan from other people, the precious life force that people create simply by virtue of living, especially if one lives one's life with passionate intensity because passion generates a lot of precious élan, or personal "virtue," simply by one's enthusiasm for life. I know, because I created a lot of "virtue" working my trade with honesty and integrity, and especially when I took up long distance running which demanded *conscious effort* and *intentional suffering.*

I generated an enormous amount of personal "virtue" living Gurdjieff's teaching and my own ethic which I borrowed, stole, or simply appropriated from *knowers* of the secret way of life like Socrates and mystics like Rumi and anyone who "spoke"' to me in that special language of the *way* that addressed my pathological need to "create" my own soul, a need, I might add, that pulled me deep into an offshoot Christian solar cult teaching that did irreparable damage to my eyesight and which I hope to write about one day in a story called "The Sunworshipper," if I can ever muster the courage to relive my experience.

By "working" on myself then, I began to see how people steal each other's élan which they need to grow in their own identity, because one needs this precious life force to satisfy the longing in their soul to become what they are meant to be, their true self; but what the self-centered shadow-afflicted person cannot see is that stolen élan must be paid for eventually, because nothing in life is free. This is the universal law of karmic accountability, and not until one sees how the reconciling law of life works will one be ready to take evolution into their own hands and complete what nature cannot finish.

If it wasn't for Gurdjieff's teaching then, I would never have acquired the sly man's secret and become aware of devil cheaters who steal élan from people to feed their own ego, like Ernest Hemingway whose selfish double needed all the élan it could get to satisfy his enormous ego, and the most abundant source of élan for Hemingway was women; hence his marriage to Hadley, Pauline, Martha, and Mary, not to mention his extra-marital relationships and foolish infatuations with young women like the beautiful Venetian aristocrat

Adriana Ivancich and the young and innocent Irish reporter Valerie Danby-Smith who went on to marry Hemingway's son Gregory and write a memoir called *Running with The Bulls*. But once he got all the élan he could get out of people, he moved on like the alpha male that he was who had to be the best at everything that he did, like marlin fishing and big game hunting, and especially writing; and he got his élan by taking obsessive control of his life to get the most satisfaction and pleasure out of life, and being clever like the devil...

46. The Books I Had to Write

Wednesday, May 24, 2017

In "Why Not Put Off Till Tomorrow the Novel You Could Begin Today?" in *Writers on Writing, Volume II,* Ann Patchett brings her essay to closure with a line that spoke directly to something I've been meaning to write about for a long time: "Sometimes if there's a book you really want to read, you have to write it yourself."

I scoured bookstores constantly when I was in hot pursuit of my true self, and I found many books (to be true, the most relevant books to my quest found me) that helped open up the secret way of life to me; but not one book, however much it moved me, including P. D. Ouspensky's *In Search of the Miraculous* that introduced me to Gurdjieff teaching, connected enough dots to provide a convincing picture of the purpose and meaning of life; and that's the book I felt I had to write after I found my true self. And I tried, book after book.

Some twenty books later I'm still trying, my most satisfying effort being my twin soul books, *Death, the Final Frontier* and *The Merciful Law of Divine Synchronicity*; but even these books fall short of the book that still wants to be set free. Maybe this is why I was called back to Hemingway again, because the book that I feel needs to be written has to be a work of fiction, not unlike Hemingway's *The Old Man and the Sea* that imaginatively transforms his hard-lived life into a simple allegory of an old man's struggling with the sea to survive with honor and dignity, idealizing one of Hemingway's favorite Spanish double sayings: *"Man can be destroyed but not defeated, defeated but not destroyed."*

Is that why he took his own life? Because he did not want life to get the best of him? Because he wanted to die on his own terms? He tells us as much in Hotchner's memoir *Papa Hemingway*; but is that Hemingway the man or Hemingway the writer speaking? He did have Santiago say in *The Old Man and the Sea,* "Man is not made for defeat." Did Hemingway take the logic of his personal dialectic to its conclusion by blowing his brains out with a double-barrelled shotgun? Where's the honor and dignity in that?

There's something to be said about a man who is true to himself, but as I learned on my own journey of self-discovery, one can be true to himself and still be false; and that seems to be the emerging quandary with my high school hero and literary mentor, because I'm beginning to see Ernest "Papa" Hemingway in a new light. Does this mean that I have a story in me that will convey the essential wisdom of my life experience the way Hemingway did in *The Old Man and the Sea*, an imaginative story of personal destiny and courage?

I don't know; but I do know that I'm being called to write a sequel to my novel *Healing with Padre Pio*. Last month Penny and I went to Orillia where the psychic medium who channelled St. Padre Pio for my novel was showing some of her craftwork at the local market. I was nudged to drive to Orillia to see her because I felt called to write a sequel to *Healing with Padre Pio*, and we made arrangements to begin this spring or early summer; but I couldn't make the commitment until we got our apartment units in our triplex up north all rented because I needed the income to take on my new literary project. (It cost one hundred and fifty-dollars a session last time, perhaps more this time.)

We lost the tenant of our upper unit two months ago, and the tenant of our middle unit was moving out in April; but we got the upper unit rented earlier this month and the new tenant for our middle unit will be moving in the first week of June, and I feel safe now paying for my monthly sessions with the psychic medium for my sequel to *Healing with Padre Pio;* but why do I feel that I *have* to write this book? What compels me?

As Ann Patchett said, "Sometimes if there's a book you really want to read, you have to write it yourself," and no one else can write this book because no one else has the kind of relationship that I established with St. Padre Pio, which I did with the ten sessions I had with my psychic medium who channelled him; but as much as I feel I have to write a sequel to *Healing with Padre Pio*, I don't think it's the book that I really HAVE to write like Hemingway HAD to write *The Old Man and the Sea* after his humiliating failure of *Across the River and into the Trees*; he HAD to redeem himself by telling the essential story of his personal and literary struggles in the parable of Santiago's incredible story.

In my call back to Hemingway then, I'm beginning to see that there is no one story that can tell the whole story of man's struggle with life; there is only one's personal story, which every writer conveys in every story they write (writers eventually come to realize that all of their stories are autobiographical in one way or another), and in my heart I *know* that I have not yet written THAT story which best conveys the essential truth of my life; that's why Ann Patchett's comment about writing the book that you want to read spoke to me.

So maybe I'm not done yet, as I thought I was. After I finished writing my twin soul books I thought I had told my story and felt satisfied; but Ann Patchett's comment stirred something in me, and I honestly feel that I'm not done yet.

I told Penny that I could die any time now and have no regrets because I did what I came here to do and written the story of my unbelievable journey of self-discovery, but I'm beginning to suspect that my call back to Hemingway was meant to inspire me to get back to creative writing so I can write the essential story of my life like Hemingway did in *The Old Man and the Sea*, an imagined story that tells the tale of my own personal struggle to find the real me. Santiago caught his fish, and I caught mine; but unlike Santiago, I brought my fish back home safe and whole, and that's my parable waiting to be written...

47. My Daimonic Novel: The Gadfly

Sunday, May 28, 2017

When it happens, it happens for a reason: this morning I was "nudged" to go online to look up Professor Harold Bloom to see if he was still with us; he's eighty-seven. I was glad to see that he still is, because I can't wait to read what may be his last book. "A big book" he said in a YouTube interview, with the working title "Possessed by Memory." But the link I went to after checking him out on Wikipedia was *Harold Bloom: New York Times,* which offered a *June 23, 2016* feature article titled "Cynthia Ozick's Long Crusade" (with Harold Bloom); and after reading this article, I read the *May 18, 2015 New York Times* book review by Cynthia Ozick on Harold Bloom's book *The Daimon Knows*, and that inspired the conversation I had with Penny this morning which reminded Penny of my novel *The Gadfly* that I had written a quarter of a century ago. Twenty-six years ago, actually.

In my last journal entry "The Books I Had to Write" I was brought to the realization, by the dialectic of the creative process that journal writing inspires, that I was called back to Hemingway again because I'm meant to write *the* story that will reflect the essential wisdom of my life-struggle like Hemingway did with his short novel *The Old Man and the Sea*; but wouldn't you know it, I believe I've already written this novel!

That's why I was nudged to look up Professor Bloom this morning, because my inner guiding principle was setting up the conditions for Penny to remind me of my novel *The Gadfly* that I had completely forgotten about; and then I dug out a copy of the manuscript that I had photo-copied and professionally bound in a printing shop in Thunder Bay so I could send it to a publisher (I wrote this on my first computer), and Penny read the first paragraph and said: *"Wow. You should be working on this novel instead of all your other stuff!"*

Here's the first paragraph of *The Gadfly*: "David Oakly puzzled the people of Springfield. He was not like everybody else. He talked little about himself, and when he volunteered information it only mystified people; like the time one of his customers insisted on knowing where he came from, he said to her: 'I come from an ancient race of mountain people who dwell beyond the ken of human thought…'"

The first paragraph drew Penny in, and I admit it drew me in also; but in all honesty, I don't remember much of this novel. How that can be, I don't know; but it was twenty-six years ago, and I did write *The Gadfly* in the grips of my *daimon*…

"What is it that the *daimon* knows?" asks Cynthia Ozick in her review of Bloom's *The Daimon Knows*. "We are meant to understand that the *daimon* is an incarnation of an intuition beyond ordinary apperception, and that this knowing lies in the halo of feeling that glows out of the language of poetry," she replies to Bloom's penetrating inquiry.

In other words, a writer's *daimon* knows much more than the writer is aware of, and abandoning to one's *daimon* gives one's creative unconscious free reign, as I did with my novel *The Gadfly* that I wrote twenty-six years ago; but even though I don't recall the story, I *know* in my heart that this is the novel that will answer my call back to Hemingway.

In *The Daimon Knows,* Bloom cites Ralph Waldo Emerson, his go-to source of Gnostic wisdom: "This is that which the strong genius works upon; the region of destiny, of aspiration, of the unknown... .Far the best part, I repeat, of every mind is not that which he knows, but that which hovers in gleams, suggestions, tantalizing unpossessed before him," which, if I may be so bold, speaks to the secret way of life that the *daimonic principle* in every writer seeks to give voice to because this is the essential wisdom of the writer's way that every writer is compelled to write, like Ernest "Papa" Hemingway was compelled to write *The Old Man and the Sea* to satisfy the unresolved *daimonic* spirit of his hard-lived life.

I feel a great relief, then. I don't have to wrestle with myself to write the essential story of my life because I've already written it; and even though I wrote it twenty-six years ago, the all-knowing creative genius of one's *daimonic* spirit speaks to the essential wisdom of the writer's way in a symbolic language that transcends time because it speaks to the eternal NOW of the secret way of life; and I can't wait to rework *The Gadfly*...

48. My Book Made Her Cry

Friday, June 2, 2017

Sharon, a retired dental assistant who heard from my neighbor Jennifer that I believed in past lives and OBEs and NDEs and all that "spiritual stuff," as Jennifer's husband called it, wanted to meet me but for two years kept putting it off, and then one day two weeks ago she was visiting Jennifer and saw me reading on my deck and they walked over and Jennifer introduced her to me, and before leaving I gave Sharon copies of my twin soul books *Death, the Final Frontier* and *The Merciful Law of Divine Synchronicity* which she read immediately, a real accomplishment because Sharon was dyslexic, and then she called to tell me that *Death, the Final Frontier* had made her cry because my book finally answered her lifelong question, *Why am I here?* and I said that we should get together and talk about it, which we did the following Sunday afternoon; and we sat on my front deck talking and talking and talking, and then Jennifer and her husband walked over and we all sat around, they sipping wine and me sherry; but I had to talk with Sharon in private again because there was something I had to ask her, and I invited her to drop over Wednesday and I learned the deeper personal reason why my book *Death, the Final Frontier* had brought her to tears.

Forty years ago, she was married to a school teacher (whom she revealed to me was a Nazi spy in his former life), and they got divorced and she married a psychologist, and together they read and studied Jane Roberts, the writer who channelled an entity called Seth; and curiously enough, I was familiar with the Seth material also because I had read Jane Roberts forty-three years ago. I know the exact date because I found the sales slip tucked between the pages of my paperback copy of Jane Roberts book *Seth Speaks,* dated *Oct. 10, 1974*; so I knew that Sharon was a seeker still looking for an answer to her question because she was now reading *The Sacred Contract* by Carolyn Myss whom I also discovered twenty years ago with her best-selling book *Anatomy of the Spirit,* and we talked about what I considered to be her best book, *Entering the Castle, Finding the Inner Path to God and Your Soul's Purpose,* because it was a perfect bridge for Sharon to my twin soul books *Death, the Final Frontier* and *The Merciful Law of Divine Synchronicity.*

"You don't need Carolyn Myss," I said to her. "Your own life is your path. If I may, did you cry as you were reading *Death, the Final Frontier?*

"No. Just at the end," Sharon said.

"The end brought you to tears?" I asked.

"Yes," she said, choking up.

"Why?" I had to ask.

"It told me why I'm here," she replied.

"It validated your life, you mean?" I asked.

"That's exactly what it did," she said, with fresh tears in her eyes.

And then we talked some more, I doing most of the talking while she listened with rapt attention as the words poured out of me and into her thirsty soul; and before she left she was so thankful for my book that answered her lifelong question that she had no more need to seek because *Death, the Final Frontier* and our long talks had convinced her that her own life was the path she was looking for, but her own life with a NEW ATTITUDE which I made a point of spelling out for her, an attitude that would change her life if she adopted an attitude of living by the virtues of the caring and unselfish life.

"Be a giver and not a taker," I summed up the new attitude of the self-transcending life of the secret way of self-reconciliation. "All spiritual paths lead to the self," I said, taking the mystery out of the quest for the purpose and meaning of one's existence. "And not until one makes their own life the path to their true self will they satisfy the longing in their soul," I continued, as she drew out of me what she needed to hear. "But it's in how one lives one's life that satisfies or doesn't satisfy one's longing for wholeness and completeness. That's the mystery of life in a nut shell, Sharon. That's what we're here for, to live our own life."

She couldn't believe it was so simple. But as simple as the mystery was, it presupposed my life's remarkable journey of self-discovery which I had distilled into my books *Death, the Final*

Frontier and *The Merciful Law of Divine Synchronicity,* and before she left I gave her copies of my books *In the Shade of the Maple Tree* and *The Man of God Walks Alone* to read because she liked how St. Padre Pio came through in *Death, the Final Frontier.*

Like my book *Death, the Final Frontier, In the Shade of the Maple Tree* and *The Man of God Walks Alone* were also an exercise in what Carl Jung called "active imagination," a series of "talks" with my creative unconscious that spoke to me through an archetypal spirit of St. Padre Pio, not unlike Neale Donald Walsch's "conversations" with God books that I had read and enjoyed and eventually outgrown; and after Sharon left I sat back and reflected on my call back to Hemingway, and in all honesty I couldn't wait to get back to creative writing because I knew that was where I was meant to be...

49. Ordinary Moments

Sunday, June 4, 2017

Yesterday morning, I posted a short story on my spiritual musings blog called "In Her Red Shorts." This story was inspired by an experience I had with a member of the spiritual community that I belonged to for over thirty years but which I withdrew from three years ago, a story that reflected the shadow side of this New Age spiritual community.

It's a story in a series of personally inspired stories that seek to reflect the principle of *enantiodromia*, and I posted it on my blog which I then shared on Twitter and Facebook. There are ten stories in this series so far, and I hope to write a few more to make a book which I'm going to publish under the title *Enantiodromia and Other Stories*. I wanted to write a novella for this book, but I'm not so sure now because I suspect the novella may evolve into a novel because I want this to be the story of my relationship with this New Age spiritual teaching that I lived for over thirty years after moving on from Gurdjieff's teaching.

In any event, when I shared my story "In Her Red Shorts" on Facebook, Penny, the love of my life and favorite reader, responded with a comment that inspired today's journal entry on what I've come to see as the secret way of life implicit to every good story. With prescient wisdom, Penny wrote: *"How magnificently the written word captures the essence of what appears to be an ordinary moment in a person's life."*

Since my return to Hemingway, I've been re-reading all my Hemingway books as well as Hemingway's short stories and novels, and yesterday I finally finished reading Carlos Baker's big biography *Ernest Hemingway: A Life Story*, and my final impression upon completing the book was that Hemingway was a selfish bastard who used and abused people; but fortunately I have enough gnostic wisdom to appreciate Hemingway's *way*, and for that I have to respect and admire the selfish bastard for having the courage to live his own life.

But this was the *enantiodromiac* nature of Hemingway's *way;* and by this I mean that it was to the inherent conflict of his selfish nature and literary integrity that spawned his complex, paradoxical personality, because in his art he sought to be true (his "one true sentence" principle and "tell it the way it was" credo), and his literary integrity threatened the false nature of his ego/shadow personality: a storm brewing to happen.

That's what defined Hemingway. His four wives (Hadley, Pauline, Martha, and Mary) called him a difficult, complicated person; but when his biographers added up the pieces of his complicated life the picture they drew was of a man who lived his life to the full so he would have all the material he needed to become the greatest writer of his generation, which some critics believed he achieved; but as he grew in literary stature, so too did his ego. And that's what made Ernest "Papa" Hemingway a self-aggrandized, selfish bastard.

In his book *Novelists and Novels*, Professor Bloom has this to say about Hemingway: "In a grand letter (September 6-7, 1949) to his publisher, Charles Scribner, he charmingly confessed, 'Am a man without ambition, except to be champion of the world. I wouldn't fight Dr. Tolstoi in a 20 round bout because I know he would knock my ears off.' This modesty passed quickly, to be followed by, 'If I can live to 60 I can beat him (MAYBE).' Since the rest of the letter counts Turgenev, de Maupassant, Henry James, even Cervantes, as well as Melville and Dostoyveski, among the defeated, we can join Hemingway, himself, in admiring his extraordinary self-confidence." If that isn't an inflated ego, what is?

But I think Bloom got it right in his belief that Hemingway was essentially "an elegiac poet who mourns the self, who celebrates the self (rather less effectively), and who suffers divisions of the self..."

After I posted my story "In Her Red Shorts" on my blog which I shared on Twitter and Facebook, Penny and I talked about story writing and Hemingway (for her morning read, Penny was reading *The View from Castle Rock* by Alice Munro), and I said to her: "I don't know what all the fuss is about. He wrote some great stories, but I think too much has been made of Hemingway. Alice Munro wrote some great stories too, which also garnered her the Nobel Prize for Literature, but what makes a story great anyway? Do you know?"

"I've told you already. I think a story has to tell you something. If a story doesn't tell you something about life, it won't leave a lasting impression. I forget them."

"I agree. A story has to get to the soul of an experience, like my experience with Jimmy Johnson at his market garden. Jimmy just had heart surgery and he's happy to be back in his little market selling fruit and vegetables. That's *his* life, his *way,* and he smiles every time a customer comes into his shop. Especially if they know him personally and exchange pleasantries. You should see the look on his face. I'd love to write a story about that."

"You want to write about everybody," Penny said, with a smile.

"No, that's not quite true. I'm only inspired to write a story when I see something in a person that speaks to *their* life. It's *their* life that interests me, and by *their* life I mean their personal, individual *way*. That's where the stories are."

That was Hemingway's literary gift, a cultivated and disciplined facility to see what Penny called "the essence of what appears to be an ordinary moment in a person's life." This "ordinary moment" is the writer's entry point into a person's *way,* the personal path of *their* individual life—whether a person is aware of it or not. But this is so difficult to explain that Hemingway called it "the secret that is poetry written into prose."

The "secret" that Hemingway caught a glimpse of in his stories is the secret way of life that is a person's individual *way,* and a writer who captures the essence of a person's *way* in what appears to be an ordinary moment has all the material he needs for a great story, like that ordinary but magical moment when Francis Macomber in Hemingway's short story "The Short Happy Life of Francis Macomber" shot the charging bull and reclaimed his courage and personal integrity that he had forfeited to his wife Margot.

In one single moment of courageous action, Francis Macomber *became* his own man, and that's what the secret way of life is all about—becoming one's own person. This is the "secret" that Hemingway saw in what appeared to be an ordinary moment in Francis Macomber's safari hunt experience when he shot that charging buffalo and salvaged his dignity. As Emily Dickinson put it: "Adventure most unto itself /The soul condemned to be; /Attended by a Single Hound— /Its own Identity."

Francis Macomber *found* his personal *way* in that magical moment and reclaimed himself, which Hemingway saw with his writer's eye, and for all of his grand-standing and brutally selfish behavior, my high school hero and literary mentor cannot be denied his genius for telling a great story. And so, I guess, maybe that's what all the fuss is about...

50. Hemingway's Destined Purpose

Monday, June 5, 2017

I wasn't going to pick up the *Sunday Star* when I pulled in for gas on the corner of Highway 92 and Concession 29 on our way home from our movie and dinner outing in Barrie yesterday (we saw the movie *Gifted,* the story of a cute little girl who happened to be a math whiz which we enjoyed immensely, and we had dinner at *East Side Mario's*, which we also enjoyed), but something prompted me to pick up the paper because my home delivery *Sunday Star* did not contain the *New York Times* and *Book Review* inserts; and, wouldn't you know it (I just love these kinds of coincidences!), the *Book Review* insert had a review of a new biography on Hemingway: *Ernest Hemingway: A Biography*, by Mary V. Dearborn, coming in at a whopping 738 pages, bigger than Carlos Baker's comprehensive tome.

It seems that my high school hero and literary mentor, whom I now dubbed a selfish bastard with a gift for writing great stories, refuses to go out of fashion; and after I read the review I went online and checked Dearborn's book out on Amazon and spent the next hour reading the lengthy Look Inside Feature, which was mostly familiar material for me given all the books I had already read on Hemingway. But because this biography was written by a woman, it offered a unique perspective on the macho world of Ernest Hemingway; and this made it interesting, to a point. Then my interest waned, because I really am getting tired of reading about Ernest Hemingway; so I doubt this book will go on my Amazon wish list.

Nevertheless, I'm going to see my call back to Hemingway to the end; which means that come hell or high water I'm going to finish reading the rest of his books so I can have a comprehensive perspective on his conflicted life and writing. But I have to ask myself, was it a coincidence that I picked up the *Sunday Star* yesterday so I could read the review of the new biography on Hemingway, or was it providentially orchestrated?

Was it a coincidence that Sherwood Anderson advised Hemingway to go to Paris instead of Italy where Ernest and his wife Hadley intended to go? Had Hemingway gone to Italy instead of Paris which helped mold him into the writer that he became, would he have succeeded like he did sans all the Paris connections that helped launch his career?

I don't think so. And this leads to the question of personal destiny, which I believe we all have, only for some people like Ernest Hemingway it's much more pronounced; and if so, what does this say about the selfish bastard that he became?

Dearborn quotes Martha Gellhorn to attest to this point of view: "A man (Hemingway) must be a very great genius to make up for being such a loathsome human being." And Hemingway's friend (whom Hemingway also betrayed), John Dos Passos wondered about the rot of Hemingway's soul when *Across the River and into the Trees* came out in 1950, "How can a man in his senses leave such garbage on the page?"

Across the River and into the Trees was savaged by the critics, using such phrases as "a thoroughly bad book," "Hemingway at his worst," and "a synthesis of everything that is bad in his previous work," but like Francis Macomber, Hemingway reclaimed his dignity with *The Old Man and the Sea* that came out two years later; and even though Professor Bloom considered Hemingway a "minor novelist with a major style" not unlike John Updike, a writer whom I happen to love for his use of *le mot juste,* I believe Hemingway broke new ground in literature with his intuitive awareness of the secret way that his stories and novels explore, which lifts him above the fray of most writers; that's why I believe that his life was orchestrated by providential design, otherwise how can one explain how he got his job writing for the *Toronto Star* which he wrote for when he and Hadley moved to Paris?

It was pure serendipity, *the merciful law of divine synchronicity* in action. When the young Hemingway came back from the war in Italy, wounded with a hero's medal, he gave what the new biographer Mary Dearborn called his "conquering-hero-home-from-the-wars speech at the Ladies Aid Society at the Petoskey Public Library," and he attracted the attention of the visiting Canadian Harriet Gridley Connable who invited the young hero to be a companion for their handicapped son Ralph Jr., a year younger than Ernest, and live in their beautiful home in Toronto while her and her husband and daughter Dorothy went on a winter vacation for several months in Palm Beach, Florida, and Harriet's husband's influence got Ernest a job reporting for the *Toronto Star*; but was that a mere coincidence, or was his career mapped out for him by Providence and his own destined purpose?

I've explored this question of free will and destined purpose in *The Merciful Law of Divine Synchronicity*, so I need not expand upon it here; but all of my re-reading on Hemingway only verifies what I already *know*—that we are free to live the life we choose to live, but we are also guided by *the omniscient guiding principle of life* which is always there to help us realize our destined purpose, as Hemingway was by all the fortunate coincidences that set him on the path to realize his dream of becoming the greatest writer of his generation, coincidences which he exploited because he was a willfully selfish, clever devil.

"This Toronto thing looks like the original Peruvian donuts," said Ernest, when offered the position of being a companion for Ralph Connable Jr., seeing a good thing when he saw one, and which serendipitously led to his writing position for the *Toronto Star.*

So, was it mere coincidence that I picked up the *Sunday Star* yesterday with the *New York Times Book Review* insert, or was I *meant* to see Mary V. Dearborn's new biography on Ernest "Papa" Hemingway, my high school hero and literary mentor?

I've experienced too many of these kinds of coincidences, especially when I'm working on a new book, to dismiss them as mere chance occurrences; they speak to the much deeper purpose of my writing life and destined purpose. Why else would I have been called back to my high school hero and literary mentor if not to get a deeper insight to his shadow-afflicted personality and get on with my own writer's *way* like Hemingway did with his?

The call to one's destined purpose never stops...

51. Hemingway's Inner Journey

Tuesday, June 6, 2017

I'm half way through my second reading of *The Hemingway Women* by Bernice Kert, and as tired as I am of reading about Hemingway's life I've connected dots that I never saw before, dots that paint a clearer picture of the great writer; almost as though I was called back to Hemingway again so I could confirm the concept of personal destiny.

"Our lives have a narrative structure, like that of novels, and at those moments we call synchronistic this structure is brought to our awareness in a way that has a significant impact on our lives," writes Robert H. Hopcke in his book *There Are No Accidents, Synchronicity and the Story of Our Lives.* And in his book *The Power of Coincidence, How Life Shows Us What We Need to Know*, David Richo writes: **"Synchronicity shows us that the world orchestrates some of our life events so they can harmonize with the requirements of our inner journey."** So as tired as I may be of reading about Hemingway's life, I've become acutely conscious of those fortuitous synchronistic events that set Ernest Hemingway on the path to his career, starting with how he got his first professional job writing for one of the best papers in America, the *Kansas City Star.*

Hemingway's parents wanted him to go to college, but Hemingway was called to his destined purpose of becoming a writer, and *the omniscient guiding principle of life* provided him with the opportunity when his father's brother Tyler Hemingway, who was successful in the lumber business in Kansas City, asked his old classmate Henry J. Haskell, chief editorial writer and Washington correspondent at the *Star,* to intercede for Ernest at the newspaper; but instead of offering him a summer job, the paper offered him a full-time job in the fall. Thus began Hemingway's apprenticeship that was to shape him into the writer he became.

One could call Hemingway's first writing job pure happenstance, but not when one connects all the other dots that set Hemingway on his path to writing; that's the pattern of his destined purpose that became clear to me the more I read about his life, and despite the freedom that Hemingway had to choose the life he wanted to live, he was always provided with serendipitous opportunities to live what David Richo called his "inner journey."

When asked by George Plimpton for *The Paris Review* if he could recall an exact moment when he wanted to become a writer, Hemingway replied: "No. I always wanted to be a writer." This was his calling. His inner journey. And although he had an outer journey like everyone else, (to get the most out of life, as Carlos Baker tells us), he was pulled to his inner journey by his call to writing; that's why he kept getting the "breaks" he did, like the "break" he got from Harriet Connable's husband whose influence got him his job at the *Toronto Star*, and the "break" he got from the strong suggestion by Sherwood Anderson, whom Hemingway had read and loved (but whom he later betrayed), to go to Paris to write instead of Italy, even writing letters of introduction for Hemingway; and his "break" when Scott Fitzgerald, who called Hemingway "the real thing," introduced him to his publisher Maxwell Perkins who launched Hemingway's career with *The Sun Also Rises*. But what made Hemingway such a difficult man was that his rapacious outer life complicated his inner journey, and in the end it finally destroyed him...

Hemingway's life has been put under the microscope, and given all the books that have been written about his life one would think that there's not much more about him that we don't already know; but more material continues to surface, like the article in *The Paris Review* by Robert K. Elder, "To Have and Have Not," dated just last month, *May 4, 2017*: "More letters shed light on Hemingway's unrequited love and early life."

Frances Elizabeth Coates and Ernest Hemingway were high-school classmates, and it seems that he was infatuated with Elizabeth. Hemingway even used a version of her name "Liz Coates" in his sexually charged 1923 story "Up in Michigan," and her name also surfaces elsewhere in his work; and according to Elder's article, Ernest wrote to Elizabeth from his hospital bed in Milan where he was healing from the wound he received by an Austrian mortar shell while serving on the Italian front as an ambulance driver for the American Red Cross, so Hemingway's love for nurse Agnes von Kurowsky, who like Elizabeth also rejected him for another man, was not his first unrequited love, which only adds to the cultish mystique that Hemingway's adventurous outer life and inner journey gave birth to.

And speaking of serendipity (those curious synchronicities that pop up out of nowhere), when I went online this morning to check my memory on Hemingway's *Paris Review* interview, I "chanced" upon Robert Elder's piece about Hemingway's unrequited love for his high school classmate Elizabeth Coates, which leads me to wonder if my call back to Hemingway hasn't been to bring me back to my own high school days when the Hemingway mystique fueled my romantic fantasy of becoming a writer like him, and my own infatuation with the girl who was to reject me like Hemingway's high-school love rejected him.

Like all the books that I've been called to write, there seems to be so much more to this journal on my writing life than meets the eye...

52. Words Matter to a Writer

Wednesday, June 7, 2017

Martha Gellhorn was a war correspondent, a seasoned journalist who also wrote short stories, novels, and memoires; words mattered to her. So, what did she mean by calling Ernest Hemingway, world-famous author and married man who left his second wife for her, a pathological liar, apocryphiar, the cruelest man she knew, and a loathsome human being?

After their divorce, Martha Gellhorn refused to talk about Ernest Hemingway because she did not consider herself an appendage to the famous writer's life; she had her own identity. That's why she left him, because Hemingway could not control her like he did his other wives; but what was it about Ernest Hemingway that fuelled her animus for him?

Words matter to a writer, and she chose her words to describe what she felt about the celebrated author whose name raised her profile, which she resented because it diminished her own identity as a writer that she worked so hard to realize; none of his other wives went on record with such contempt. Hadley, Hemingway's first wife, chose her words with caution when speaking about him; Pauline vented her spleen, but not with the vitriolic contempt that Martha Gellhorn had for him; and his fourth wife Mary finally gave her version of her long-suffering marriage in her memoir *How It Was*; but only Martha, the only one of his four wives to walk away from him, vexed the beast that lurked in Hemingway's heart. Why?

Pathological liar, apocryphiar, cruelest man she knew, and loathsome human being are very harsh words; they cut to the core of one's *being*. Or one's *non-being*, to be precise; and Hemingway's false self (the demons that made up his ego/shadow personality) had taken on its own identity by the time Martha first met him in *Sloppy Joe's* bar in Key West, Florida, and after their protracted affair and tempestuous marriage she could no longer suffer Hemingway's dark shadow personality, and for her peace of mind had to leave him.

Martha Gellhorn's personal freedom was much too precious to forfeit to a brutally selfish egocentric given to bouts of depression and megalomania; that's the final impression that all of the reading I've done on Hemingway's life and writing these past few months has left me with and which helped me to see more clearly how my high school hero and literary mentor could become so contemptable to those who experienced his dark side.

But is it fair of me to talk about Hemingway this way? I'm not a psychiatrist or Jungian analyst, nor a scholar on Hemingway's life; I'm just a little-known writer from Georgian Bay, Southcentral Ontario, and my only claim to understanding Hemingway would be my gnostic awareness of the shadow side of life and the secret way of literature.

Words matter to me also, and I don't use them lightly; so, I take Martha Gellhorn at her word when she called Hemingway a pathological liar, apocryphiar, the cruelest man she knew, and a loathsome human being. Which isn't to say that Hemingway didn't have a good and fair and kind and honest and compassionate sensitive side, or why else would she and three other women have married him? But because Hemingway had a larger-than-life personality, he also had a larger-than-life dark side which she experienced up close.

That's what made Hemingway such a complicated person who continues to fascinate the world, myself especially because in him I see life writ large; that's why I was called to write *The Lion that Swallowed Hemingway* three years ago, and now this journal/sequel with a deeper insight into the paradoxical personality of my high school hero and literary mentor.

I've grown in gnostic awareness since I wrote *The Lion that Swallowed Hemingway,* and I hope I have offered a deeper psycho/literary insight into the *enantiodromiac* nature of Hemingway's ego/shadow personality, which may well be the essential reason I was called back to him; but in all honesty, as much antipathy as I still have for Ernest Hemingway l am no less respectful of his courage to jump into the stream of life and live it to the full so he could write about it. That was Hemingway's destined purpose, and what he gave to the world in his short stories and novels have become an invaluable legacy to *the living way of literature.*

EPILOGUE

My Own Summing Up

What a relief, to have resolved my lifelong fascination with Ernest "Papa" Hemingway who called me to writing in high school, a lingering fascination which I thought I had finally put to rest when I wrote *The Lion that Swallowed Hemingway* three years ago but which returned full force when I was called back to my high school hero and literary mentor with the gift of an *Indigo Hemingway Notebook* last Christmas that inspired my journal/sequel to my memoir, but when I brought my reflections on Hemingway to closure with my final entry "Words Matter to a Writer" (*Wednesday, June 7, 2017*), I was nudged to read Somerset Maugham's memoir *The Summing Up* again. I couldn't fathom why I felt nudged to reread Maugham's memoir until I made the connection between my fascination with the man who called me to writing and the man who wrote *The Razor's Edge* that inflicted me with the immortal wound that sparked the fire in my soul to become a seeker like Maugham's hero Larry Darrell, two famous writers who had an enormous influence upon my life for which I am eternally grateful; but as I delved into *The Summing Up* again I felt a growing sense of resolution for the obligation I felt I had to the writer whose novel inflicted me with the immortal wound that overrode my call to writing, and when I finished reading *The Summing Up* I took out Maugham's novel *The Razor's Edge* to read again, for the third time because I had read it again ten or twelve years ago just to see how it read from the perspective of having satisfied the longing in my soul, a longing that drove Hemingway to suicide and Maugham into the darkest corner of his soul. "I neither believe in immortality nor desire it," he summed up. "I should like to die quietly and painlessly, and I am content to be assured that with my last breath, my soul, with its aspirations and its weaknesses will dissolve into nothingness."

I felt like crying when I read those words, I had so much respect for the author of *The Razor's Edge*; but I could not cry, because the truth of Somerset Maugham's *way*, however idiosyncratic and alluring, had freely brought him to an impasse that he could not resolve, and with a comfortable but disquieting sense of resignation he begins his foray into what he called neither an autobiography nor a book of reflections, but merely a summing up of his life: "Everything I say is merely an opinion of my own. The reader can take it or leave it. If he has any patience to read what follows he will see that there is only one thing about which I am certain, and this is that there is very little about which one can be certain."

Like many writers who presume a knowledge they do not have, Maugham could not possibly know that there is very little about which one can be certain, because there are many things of which I have become certain in my quest for my true self, and one gnostic certainty in particular speaks to both Ernest "Papa" Hemingway and William Somerset Maugham, who were both burdened by the oppressive spirit of nihilism: *life is a journey through vanity to humility*, and not until we have been humbled enough by life to become what we are meant to be and realize our true nature will we be free of the doubt and uncertainty that comes with the *enantiodromiac* process of our becoming.

I spent several days on my front deck reading *The Summing Up,* enjoying it no less the third time as I did the first and second, and another day on the deck reading *A Traveller in Romance, Uncollected Writings 1901-1964*, by W. Somerset Maugham, and I enjoyed this for the third time as well; that's how much I love reading Maugham's personal writing. And I also reread "Extracts from *A Writer's Notebook*" in *Mr. Maugham Himself*, by W. Somerset Maugham, selected by John Beecroft (I still love his story "The Buried Talent," which is one of the most moving portraits of the unlived life I have ever read), and then I went on YouTube and listened to Professor Robert Calder on how he came to write his biography on Somerset Maugham, and then I listened to Maugham himself on YouTube; but he's more enjoyable to read than listen to because he comes across as life-weary and depressingly dour.

A masterful storyteller, Maugham was a superb craftsman who used words like a portrait artist uses the various shades of colour to paint a picture of his subjects, and so effectively did Maugham draw his characters—physically, emotionally, intellectually, and spiritually—that he seduces the reader into believing his portraitures;

that's what made him such a popular writer read by millions. "I cannot help thinking that to entertain is sufficient ambition for a novelist, and it is certainly one which is hard to achieve; if he can tell a good story and create characters that are fresh and living he has done enough to make the reader grateful," he wrote in *A Traveller in Romance*. But when I read his story "Red," for the third time because something felt askew about this story, the bubble of his story's reality burst and I saw through his masterful technique of storytelling, because the portrait that he drew of his protagonist Red seriously challenged my credulity. *"Wow,"* I said to myself, when the hypnotic spell broke during my third reading. *"He painted such a convincing picture of Red's life that he seduced me into believing him. That's incredible writing!"*

And that's exactly what he did with his novel *The Razor's Edge,* seducing me into believing that the story *actually* happened as he told it. Maugham himself plays the most vital role in the novel, the innocuous narrator of the story that he shares with his readers, telling us in chapter one (like the consummate gossiper that I finally discerned him to be): "Many years ago I wrote a novel called *The Moon and Sixpence*. In this book, I took a famous painter, Paul Gauguin, and, using the novelist's privilege, devised a number of incidents to illustrate the character I had created on the suggestion afforded me by the scanty facts that I knew about the French artist. ***In the present book I have attempted to do nothing of the kind. I have invented nothing.***" The bold italics are mine; and then Maugham the narrator tells us that he made up the names of his characters to not embarrass the people still living, which created such a strong impression upon my credulous young mind that it went a long way to inflicting that deadly immortal wound upon my soul which called me to my true self.

Masterful, masterful storytelling. But what made William Somerset Maugham such a masterful storyteller was also the clarity of his writing, the product of a disciplined aesthetic of writing with "lucidity, simplicity, and euphony," plus his uncanny understanding of human nature, which he spells out in *The Summing Up*: "I have never seen people all of one piece. It has amazed me that the most incongruous traits should exist in the same person and for all that yield a plausible harmony. I have often asked myself how characteristics, seemingly irreconcilable, can exist in the same person...Selfishness and kindliness, idealism and sensuality, vanity, shyness, disinterestedness, courage, laziness, nervousness, obstinacy, and diffidence, they can all exist in a single person and form a plausible harmony. It has taken a long time to persuade readers of the truth of this."

Maugham had the writer's gift of seeing the shadow side of human nature, an uncanny talent that he cultivated and mastered over many decades of disciplined writing. He wrote *The Summing Up* when he was only sixty-four, thinking that he was coming to the end of his life, and he had not yet written the novel that inflicted the immortal wound upon my soul that called me to my destined purpose; he wrote *The Razor's Edge* in his early seventies, and he went on to live to the ripe old age of ninety-one. A long, long life which he did not want to repeat, as he shares with us in *The Summing Up*: "I have been asked on occasion whether I would be willing to live my life over again. On the whole it has been a pretty good one, perhaps better than that of most people, but I should see no point in repeating it. It would be as idle as to read again a detective story that you have read before. But supposing there were such a thing as reincarnation...I might enjoy experiences which circumstances and my own idiosyncrasies, spiritual and corporeal, have prevented me from enjoying and learn the many things that I have not had the time or opportunity to learn. But now I should refuse. I have had enough. There are indeed days when I feel that I have done everything too often, known too many people, read too many books, seen too many pictures, statues, churches and fine houses, and listened to too much music. I neither believe in immorality nor desire it. I should like to die quietly and painlessly, and I am content to be assured that with my last breath, my soul, with its aspirations and its weaknesses, will dissolve into nothingness."

There we have it, then; a thoughtful, reasonable, exceptionally well-read and travelled man who diligently explored the meaning and purpose of life in the literature, religions, and philosophies of the world and came up empty-handed, a man whose wealth gave him a "sixth sense" to indulge and enjoy his other five senses, a hedonist who got all the pleasure out of life that he could manage (he was a homosexual, which he kept from the public his whole life to safeguard his image for his millions of readers) but whose life by his own admission in the end would dissolve into nothingness. A "useless passion" condemned by his freedom to choose his own values in a world that was ultimately meaningless and absurd, as Sartre would say; but not for me and many of his readers who were moved by his stories.

It's ironic then that *The Razor's Edge* that called me to my destined purpose was written by a man who did not believe in God, an immortal soul, or afterlife; but that was his *way*, his personal path that he wrought out of life. Somerset Maugham did not kowtow to any religion, philosophy, or ideology; he made up his own mind on everything, which I admired and enjoyed in how he reflected it in his writing, quite often with an ironic sense of humor.

But what I loved most about Somerset Maugham was the strange effect his writing had upon me, like I was secretly listening in on privileged gossip. I could never put my finger on what it was about his writing that I liked so much (apart from masterful storytelling), but as I read *The Summing Up* on my front deck for the third time it came to me, and rather than go upstairs to get my *Hemingway Notebook* I jotted my feelings down in one of the blank pages at the back of the book: *"Maugham is the consummate gossiper. He gossips about life with the eloquence of a gifted talker. He has the gift of catching your attention to the juicy bits of life and fills your ears with the delicate salaciousness that gossip has to offer. **He satisfies an unspoken prurient need in the reader to see into the private lives of people.**"*

And he as much as admitted to this masterful technique of storytelling (I don't know what to call it, really; maybe "whoring") by telling us in *The Summing Up* that he was basically a shy person (he had a self-conscious stammer his whole life) who relied upon his life partner/secretary Alan Searle for the latest bits of juicy gossip that he picked up from people in the exclusive circles they travelled in which he later used ("pandered") in his novels and stories, like he did in *The Razor's Edge* which seduced me with the voluptuous ease of an accomplished whore making love to an innocent schoolboy; but then, isn't that what fiction is all about—giving us a privileged glimpse into the private corners of life?

Maugham was no different than other writers, only eminently much more masterful; but something was missing in his writing, something which I found in my high school hero and literary mentor Ernest "Papa" Hemingway, something that satisfied me much more than my prurient need to see into the private lives of people, the more private the more satisfying, something different and more alluring, something that spoke to my soul...

Everyone loves a good story. It's to our nature. It's how information was passed on to the tribe as our ancestors sat around the open fire listening to stories. Carl Jung's psychology of the individuation process sprang from the seed of his most important discovery about story, which came to him as he listened with compassion and patience to his mental patients in the Burgholzli psychiatric hospital in Zurich during his ten-year internship.

"Jung said that he learned from the start how in every disturbance of the personality, even in its most extreme psychotic form of schizophrenia, or dementia praecox as it was then called, one could discern the elements of a personal story. *The story was the personality's most precious possession*, whether it knew it or not, and the person could only be cured or healed by the psychiatrist getting hold of the story," wrote Jung's friend Laurens van der Post in his remarkable memoir *Jung and the Story of Our Time*.

Jung came to the breakthrough realization that "the arrest of the personality in one profound unconscious timeless moment of itself called psychosis, occurred because the development of the person's story had been interrupted, however varied, individual, and numerous the causes of the interruption," wrote Laurens van der Post; and Jung came to see that the only way to heal his patients was to help them reconnect with their life story, which is why he said in an interview many years after he left the Burgholzli and had worked out the *enantiodromiac* dynamic of the secret way of life into his psychology of the individuation process: *"As each plant grows from a seed and becomes in the end an oak tree, so man must become what he is meant to be. He ought to get there, but most get stuck,"*

Getting souls unstuck was Jung's lifelong mission, which he did directly and indirectly through his practice (he saw up to eight patients a day for decades and analyzed over eighty thousand dreams over his lifetime) and the many books that he wrote which helped countless people like myself get unstuck from our mindsets, and also by being the inspiration for the founding of Alcoholics Anonymous which has been a blessing for many people.

Laurens van der Post, who grew up in Africa and was well acquainted with the Bushmen, the first people of South Africa "who were perhaps the greatest story-tellers Africa had ever known," told Jung that the Bushmen passed on their knowledge through story, that "story was the seed and essence of their history, their present and future," and through the Bushmen he came to realise that "without a story of its own no culture, society, or personality could survive." Upon this realization, Jung developed his psychology of individuation.

So, story is in our genes because we *are* our own story, and telling stories is how we pass on the *meaning* of life. This is the *daimonic imperative* of storytelling, the mystical pull that compels writers to write stories and pass on the meaning of life, and why readers read stories to satisfy their inherent need to know the meaning of their own life's purpose.

Essentially this was the theme of my twin soul book *The Merciful Law of Divine Synchronicity,* which told my story of how *the omniscient guiding principle of life* always came to my aid whenever my own life story got interrupted; so my understanding of story goes beyond the horizons of Literature 101, because what it took to reconnect with my personal story—what Jung came to call one's personal myth—cost me more than most people are willing to pay (hence my memoir *The Pearl of Great Price*), which is why I feel as I do about Ernest "Papa" Hemingway and William Somerset Maugham.

Hemingway called me to writing and Maugham's novel *The Razor's Edge* supplanted my call to writing by inflicting me with the immortal wound that compelled me to become a seeker like Larry Darrell in Maugham's novel, and after years of *conscious individuation* with Gurdjieff's teaching, the sayings of Jesus, and my personal ethic I realized my true self and was free to return to creative writing; but in my return I brought something that neither Hemingway nor Maugham had realized about storytelling—that story *is* who we are; or, as Marshal McLuhan expressed this mystical insight, *"the medium is the message."*

This is why I said to Sharon, the woman who cried when she read my twin soul books when we were sitting on my front deck talking: "It's not, what is the point of the story? The story *is* the point. That's why you cried when you came to the end of my book *Death, the Final Frontier*. You got the point of my story because *I am the point of my story*, and the meaning of my life story resonated with you so much that it moved you to tears of relief."

My personal story "spoke" to Sharon's soul, and she "heard" what she needed to hear to answer her lifelong question, *"Why am I here?"* My story awakened her to herself, and that relieved her of the burden of seeking; that's why she cried. And she reflected her feelings in her Amazon review of my book *The Spiritual Law of Divine Synchronicity*: "I have been on my spiritual quest for over 36 years. I started with Jane Roberts "Seth Speaks" and his teachings. I have just finished reading this book and "Death, the Final Frontier" by you. I was so moved and in tune with your teachings that I cried after reading them. Thank you Orest, for helping me on my journey. I am continuing on my path of enlightenment from you and your books. I can now see the sky through the trees and I will go on."

We are all looking for the answer to our life's purpose, but very few of us realize that our own life *is* the purpose of our life; this is what Victor Frankl realized with his book *Man's Search for Meaning*. It's not what we expect from life that answers the question to our life's purpose, but what life expects of us; and what life expects of us is to *live* our own life, because our own life *is* the way to our true self, which fulfills life's purpose.

In the shortest terms possible, life expects us to realize our true self which we can only do by *becoming* our true self; and we can only *become* our true self by taking evolution into our own hands to complete what nature cannot finish. This is the mystery that stumps everyone, Hemingway and Maugham included; but by adopting the *right attitude* we can satisfy the longing in our soul and meet life's expectations. "The salvation of man is through love and in love," said Victor Frankl; and Doctor Elisabeth Kubler-Ross's life story brought her to the same conclusion, which she shared in her memoir *The*

Wheel of Life, A Memoir of Living and Dying: "All destiny leads down the same path—growth, love and service."

This is what was missing in Maugham's stories, the gnostic wisdom that our own life *is* the way to satisfy the longing in our soul for wholeness and completeness, which Hemingway captured best in "The Short Happy Life of Francis Macomber" and "The Snows of Kilimanjaro," two stories that reveal how the natural *enantiodromiac* process of life affected the protagonists of both stories, Francis Macomber redeeming himself from himself and the failed writer Harry facing his mortality and coming to the realization that he had squandered his talent for the good life that the wealthy women in his life afforded him.

Ernest "Papa" Hemingway sought redemption through writing for his tortured and conflicted soul, and William Somerset Maugham, who didn't believe there was anything to be saved from, got the most out of his life that he could get, as he tells us on his 90th birthday: "Somewhat early, but at what age I cannot remember, I made up my mind that, having but one life, I should like to get the most I could out of it. I wanted to make a pattern of my life, in which writing would be an essential element, but which would include all other activities proper to man, and which death in the end would round off in complete fulfillment."

Hemingway also got the most out of life that he could get, but the difference between my high school hero and literary mentor and the man who wrote *The Razor's Edge* was that Hemingway wrote to save himself from himself and Maugham wrote to entertain his readers and make more money to support his lavish, hedonistic lifestyle (he owned a villa in the south of France where he entertained the rich and famous); that's why the critics maintained that Somerset Maugham was a master craftsman and not an artist, which irritated the hell out of him because he could not see that his stories did not aspire to the lofty heights of art, which Karen Blixen defined as "the truth above the facts of life."

Hemingway sought the truth above the facts of life, "the secret that is poetry written into prose" which he saw in Cezanne's paintings; and Maugham believed that the facts of life were all there was, which he wrote about in the most entertaining manner possible to sell more books and add to his coffers, like a clever artist painting portraits *just to please his readers*; but, if I may end my own summing up on a point of irony, which I'm sure Maugham would appreciate, the man who wrote *The Razor's Edge* could not see that Larry Darrell's story *was* the point of the novel, which is why it inflicted me with the immortal wound that set my soul on fire and launched me on my quest for my true self. And now, as the saying goes, I can put Ernest Hemingway and Somerset Maugham to bed.

———

ALSO BY OREST STOCCO

POETRY

Not My Circus, Not My Monkeys

NOVELS

The Golden Seed
Tea with Grace
Jesus Wears Dockers
Healing with Padre Pio
Keeper of the Flame
My Unborn Child
On the Wings of Habitat
What Would I Say Today If I Were to Die Tomorrow?

NON-FICTION

Death, the Final Frontier
The Merciful Law of Divine Synchronicity
Gurdjieff Was Wrong But His Teaching Works
The Man of God Walks Alone
The Summoning of Noman
The Lion that Swallowed Hemingway
The Sum of All Spiritual Paths
Do We Have An Immortal Soul?
Stupidity Is Not a Gift of God
Letters to Padre Pio
Old Whore Life
Just Going with the Flow
Why Bother? The Riddle of the Good Samaritan
The Pearl of Great Price
In The Shade of the Maple Tree

About the Author

Born with a spiritual restlessness that could not be tamed by my Christian faith, I became a spiritual seeker when I discovered reincarnation in Plato's Dialogues at the age of fifteen. I grew up in a small town in Northwestern Ontario, and at twenty-one I had my own pool hall and vending machine business, but my restless spirit called me away to seek out my destiny, and I sold my business and sailed to France.

In the Alpine city of Annecy, in the Haute-Savoie region of France I had a dream that called me to my destiny. I entered into the mind of every person in the world and took every question they had ever asked and reduced them all to one question: *Why am I?* I returned to Canada and went to university to study philosophy to seek an answer to this haunting question, and by "chance" I discovered Gurdjieff, the redoubtable teacher of a system of transformative thought that he called "the Work." His Teaching excited my restless spirit and compelled me to seek out the answer to man's disquieting question in the fast, often tumultuous currents of daily living.

Visit him at: http://ostocco.wix.com/ostocco
Spiritual Musings Blog:
http://www.spiritualmusingsbyoreststocco.blogspot.com

www.ingramcontent.com/pod-product-compliance
Lightning Source LLC
Chambersburg PA
CBHW021052090426
42738CB00006B/310